REVISE BTEC NATIONAL
Sport
UNITS 19 AND 22

REVISION GUIDE

Series Consultant: Harry Smith

Authors: Layla Hall, Sonia Lal and Chris Manley

A note from the publisher

While the publishers have made every attempt to ensure that advice on the qualification and its assessment is accurate, the official specification and associated assessment guidance materials are the only authoritative source of information and should always be referred to for definitive guidance.

This qualification is reviewed on a regular basis and may be updated in the future. Any such updates that affect the content of this Revision Guide will be outlined at **www.pearsonfe.co.uk/BTECchanges**. The eBook version of this Revision Guide will also be updated to reflect the latest guidance as soon as possible.

For the full range of Pearson revision titles across KS2, KS3, GCSE, Functional Skills, AS/A Level and BTEC visit:
www.pearsonschools.co.uk/revise

Published by Pearson Education Limited, 80 Strand, London, WC2R 0RL.

www.pearsonschoolsandfecolleges.co.uk

Copies of official specifications for all Pearson qualifications may be found on the website: qualifications.pearson.com

Text and illustrations © Pearson Education Limited 2017
Typeset and illustrated by Kamae Design, Oxford
Produced by Out of House Publishing
Cover illustration by Eoin Coveney

The rights of Layla Hall, Sonia Lal and Chris Manley to be identified as authors of this work have been asserted by them in accordance with the Copyright, Designs and Patents Act 1988.

First published 2017

20 19
10 9 8 7 6 5 4

British Library Cataloguing in Publication Data
A catalogue record for this book is available from the British Library

ISBN 978 1 292 22164 9

Printed in Italy by L.E.G.O. S.p.A.

Acknowledgements
The authors and publisher would like to thank the following individuals and organisations for their kind permission to reproduce copyright material.

Text on page 69 Football Whispers Press Office, May 2017.

Photographs
(Key: b-bottom; c-centre; l-left; r-right; t-top)

123RF: Graham Oliver 07, Karel Joseph Noppe Brooks 08, Nito500 48, Tyler Olson 50, Donato Fiorentino 52, Goodluz 55l, Tatiana Belova 55r, Antonio Balaguer Soler 58, Luckybusiness 60, Vereshchagin Dmitry 61l, Stylephotographs 61r, Auremar 62, mipan 65; **Alamy Stock Photo:** Bob Daemmrich 02, Dennis MacDonald/aAGE footstock 03l, Jonathan Larsen/Diadem Images 04t, John Birdsall 04bl, Michael Dunlea 04br, John Fryer 05r, Mark Richardson 06, Athol Pictures 09, Paul Riddle/View Pictures Ltd 16, Martin Apps 18, Aflo Co. Ltd. 21, batch first collection 25t, Sport In Pictures 026, Wenn Ltd 42, 47r, ZUMA Press, Inc. 43, Keith Morris 45, Johner Images 47l, Geoffrey Robinson 56, Allstar Picture Library 59t, Tribune Content Agency LLC 59b; **Fotolia:** ARochau 01t, **Getty Images:** Technotr/E+ 01b, Julian Finney 03r, Marwan Naamani 05l, Christopher Lee 24, Lindsey Parnaby 25b; **Shutterstock:** Frantic00 17, Natursports 20, Arek Malang 49t, Kzenon 49b, LightField Studios 53; **Sport England-This Girl Can:** 12

All other images © Pearson Education

Notes from the publisher

1. While the publishers have made every attempt to ensure that advice on the qualification and its assessment is accurate, the official specification and associated assessment guidance materials are the only authoritative source of information and should always be referred to for definitive guidance.

Pearson examiners have not contributed to any sections in this resource relevant to examination papers for which they have responsibility.

2. Pearson has robust editorial processes, including answer and fact checks, to ensure the accuracy of the content in this publication, and every effort is made to ensure this publication is free of errors. We are, however, only human, and occasionally errors do occur. Pearson is not liable for any misunderstandings that arise as a result of errors in this publication, but it is our priority to ensure that the content is accurate. If you spot an error, please do contact us at resourcescorrections@pearson.com so we can make sure it is corrected.

Websites

Pearson Education Limited is not responsible for the content of any external internet sites. It is essential for tutors to preview each website before using it in class so as to ensure that the URL is still accurate, relevant and appropriate. We suggest that tutors bookmark useful websites and consider enabling students to access them through the school/college intranet.

Introduction

Which units should you revise?

This Revision Guide has been designed to support you in preparing for the externally assessed units of your course. Remember that you won't necessarily be studying all the units included here — it will depend on the qualification you are taking.

BTEC National Qualification	Externally assessed units
Diploma	1 Anatomy and Physiology 2 Fitness Training and Programming for Health, Sport and Well-being 22 Investigating Business in the Sport and Active Leisure Industry
Extended Diploma	1 Anatomy and Physiology 2 Fitness Training and Programming for Health, Sport and Well-being 19 Development and Provision of Sport and Physical Activity 22 Investigating Business in the Sport and Active Leisure Industry

You can revise Units 1 and 2 using a separate Revision Guide and its accompanying Revision Workbook, both also available from Pearson:

- Revise BTEC National Sport Units 1 and 2 Revision Guide (ISBN 978 1 292 23053 5)
- Revise BTEC National Sport Units 1 and 2 Revision Workbook (ISBN 978 1 292 23060 3).

Visit www.pearsonschools.co.uk/revise for more information.

Your Revision Guide

Each unit in this Revision Guide contains two types of pages, shown below.

Content pages help you revise the essential content you need to know for each unit.

Skills pages help you prepare for your exam or assessed task. Skills pages have a coloured edge and are shaded in the table of contents.

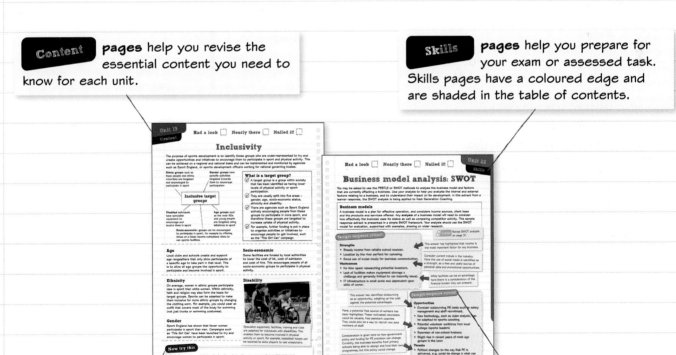

Use the **Now try this** activities on every page to help you test your knowledge and practise the relevant skills.

Look out for the **example student responses** to exam questions or set tasks on the skills pages. Post-its will explain their strengths and weaknesses.

Contents

A small bit of small print
Pearson publishes Sample Assessment Material and the Specification on its website. This is the official content and this book should be used in conjunction with it. The questions in *Now try this* have been written to help you test your knowledge and skills. Remember: the real assessment may not look like this.

Participation

Participation in sport can be recreational, competitive or professional, and people can participate in various roles.

Roles in sport

You can be involved in sport in a number of different roles.

- **Performer** – someone who takes part in the sport at any level.
- **Official** – a person who enforces the rules and regulations of the activity.
- **Administrator** – an individual who organises and administers business on someone else's behalf.
- **Volunteer** – someone, whether it be in a coaching, officiating or an administrative role, who does not get paid yet will still help with the running and organisation of the sporting activity. For instance, this could be someone who gave their time up to volunteer in the London Olympics 2012.
- **Coach** – a person who trains and encourages performers in the sport.

Recreational sport

Sport can be played in a recreational manner.

People play recreational sport for a number of reasons. People play for **fun**, often without a competitive element. Individuals enjoy **socialising** with friends to play sport or become involved in a sporting activity in their own time, such as being a member of a running club.

Competitive sport

People may participate in sport for **competitive** reasons. From social recreational football leagues such as adult five-a-side football to professional footballers being paid huge sums of money, people can gain multiple benefits from playing competitive sport. Participating in sport can teach children how to compete in the real world, such as in school and later on at work. Playing sport competitively at school or in a local club is also the first step to competition at the highest level.

Professional sport

Some people can become **professional** performers – whereby playing sport is a paid career, rather than playing as an **amateur**. For example, professional boxers box as a full-time job and are paid to fight by the sponsoring organisation, whereas amateurs can pursue other jobs while participating in relevant events. Other people participating in a professional manner may include doctors and physiotherapists who may be employed by a team to look after the athletes.

A professional performer and professional coach.

Now try this

1. Why do you think individuals volunteer their time to participate in sport?
2. With a friend, can you name individuals who participate recreationally, competitively and professionally?

1

Inclusivity

The purpose of sports development is to identify those groups who are under-represented to try and create opportunities and initiatives to encourage them to participate in sport and physical activity. This can be achieved on a regional and national basis and can be implemented and monitored by agencies such as Sport England, or sports development officers working for national governing bodies.

Ethnic groups such as black people and ethnic minorities are targeted and encouraged to participate in sport

Gender groups have specific activities targeted towards them to encourage participation

Inclusive target groups

Disabled individuals have specialist equipment to encourage and involve them in sport

Age groups such as the over 50s and young people are targeted using initiatives in sport

Socio-economic: groups can be encouraged to participate in sport, for example by offering those on a lower income subsidised rates to use sports facilities

What is a target group?

✓ A target group is a group within society that has been identified as having lower levels of physical activity or sport participation.

✓ They are usually split into five areas – gender, age, socio-economic status, ethnicity and disability.

✓ There are agencies such as Sport England actively encouraging people from these groups to participate in more sport, and therefore these groups are targeted to increase uptake of physical activity.

✓ For example, further funding is put in place to organise activities or initiatives to encourage people to get involved, such as the 'This Girl Can' campaign.

Age

Local clubs and schools create and support age ranges/tiers that only allow participants of a specific age to take part in that level. This is to allow all age groups the opportunity to participate and become involved in sport.

Socio-economic

Some facilities are funded by local authorities to lower the cost of kit, cost of admission and cost of hire. This encourages people of all socio-economic groups to participate in physical activity.

Ethnicity

On average, women in ethnic groups participate less in sport than white women. Within ethnicity, faith and religion may also form the basis for target groups. Sports can be adapted to make them inclusive for more ethnic groups by changing the clothing worn. For example, you could wear an outfit that covers most of the body for swimming (not just trunks or swimming costumes).

Gender

Sport England has shown that fewer women participate in sport than men. Campaigns such as 'This Girl Can' have been launched to try and encourage women to participate in sport.

Disability

Specialist equipment, facilities, training and rules are adapted for individuals with disabilities. This enables them to become involved in physical activity or sport. For example, basketball hoops can be lowered to allow players to use wheelchairs.

Now try this

Think of any government initiatives that have been designed to encourage people to participate in sport or physical activity.

Progression along the sports development continuum

A key function of sports development is to help individuals progress through the **sports development continuum**. This is a model that represents **four levels** of sporting participation, and shows how an individual can progress to become an elite performer.

The sports development continuum

Excellence ① — This stage represents the small number of performers who achieve excellence. This level includes elite athletes, professionals and those at an international level.

Performance ② — At the performance stage, a sportsperson will train regularly with a good coach to develop their skills and technique. They are competing at a high standard, such as club or county level.

Participation ③ — At this level, people participate regularly for enjoyment. At this stage a performer may become part of a local team or club.

Foundation ④ — This stage is made up of people who are beginners at the sport, such as young children. Participants at this level are still developing basic skills and movements.

The sports development continuum is represented by a pyramid as the large number of participants at the lower levels tapers up to a smaller number of excellent performers at the top.

Progression along the continuum

Athletes can progress along the continuum if their talent is noticed by scouts or if they are selected for a programme such as UK Sport's Talent ID. The role of Talent ID is to spot athletes with the potential to progress to an elite level. Organisations may invite athletes with certain characteristics (over a certain height, a certain age, gender or talented at a particular sport) to apply for the Talent ID programmes. Experienced coaches and support staff will help develop the athlete to progress to the excellence level.

Elite players at the **excellence** level may train for 20 hours per week, and receive funding from a sponsor, or (for tennis) from the Lawn Tennis Association.

This primary school PE lesson shows tennis players at the **foundation** stage.

Now try this

1   Describe **one** characteristic of an individual who participates in football at the performance stage.

2   Choose a sport you participate in. Identify where you are on the development continuum for that sport, and justify your answer.

 For number 2, try to give concrete examples that directly relate to the sport to explain your level.

3

Gender, age and socio-economic barriers

Barriers to participation prevent people from regularly taking part in sport and active leisure activities. These barriers are grouped into five factors, or target groups, which impact upon participation: gender, age, socio-economic, ethnicity and disability (see also page 5 for more on ethnicity and disability barriers).

1 Gender

Some sports teams are for men or women only. Sports are not always available equally to both sexes. Traditional views of women as child carers may prevent participation in sport. Gender stereotyping can also prevent people from taking part in some sports activities. Culturally, sports may be seen as male- or female-only, which reduces participation from the opposite sex.

2 Age

Older people may find it difficult to find activities suitable for them to participate in. The activity may be **inaccessible** or too **physically demanding**. Younger people rely on **parents for transport** and **supervision** at sports activities. Everyone, no matter their age, should be able to be active to some degree.

3 Socio-economic

Some people may have a **lack** of **disposable income** to spend on sports activities. They may be unaware of the variety of sports available and be unable to afford to try certain sports owing to the cost of equipment and clothing. For example certain sports are expensive to participate in, such as golf, polo and horse riding. In addition, people of a lower socio-economic status may work long hours and have responsibilities such as childcare, which mean they don't have free time to play sports.

Now try this

1 Describe **one** barrier that has prevented you from taking part in sports activities.
2 What other sports have barriers that can limit people from a poor socio-economic background from participating?

Ethnicity and disability barriers

Barriers to participation prevent people from regularly taking part in sport and active leisure activities.

④ Ethnicity

People from certain ethnic backgrounds may have religious and cultural differences which can be a barrier to participation. For example, for religious reasons some Muslim women prefer to be covered and not mix with men, which could prevent participation in mixed sessions.

The Active People Survey 2011–2012 showed that participation varied greatly by ethnic group. Among women in particular there was a large difference between white female participation (31%) and Asian female participation (21%). According to a Sport England survey in 2000, a large proportion of individuals from all ethnic groups say that they would like to take up a sport in which they currently do not participate. 'Home and family responsibilities' was a particularly common reason stated for not taking part among the Indian and Bangladeshi communities especially.

Multiple barriers

People may not be able to join in with sports activities for a number of reasons.

Participants can fall into more than one group, such as a disabled Muslim woman or an older, visually-impaired man.

⑤ Disability

People with disabilities may face a number of issues preventing their participation in some sports activities.

- There may be a lack of specialised equipment to enable physically disabled people to participate.
- There may also be a lack of clubs or facilities that disabled people are able to attend, such as wheelchair basketball clubs.
- There has been a large increase in funding and government interest in disability in sport in the UK. For example, the Paralympic World Class Performance Programme increased its funding to £73 million in 2016 from £10 million in 2000.

Remember not all disability is classed as physical. For example, those with a sensory impairment (hearing or sight loss) are also included in this bracket. There are also different levels of disability, and this is evident in events such as the Paralympics when athletes are classed into groups to compete against one another. For example, a swimmer with one leg may compete against a swimmer who has both legs but minimal movement.

Now try this

1   Choose a sport you participate in. Identify the possible barriers to participation.
2   Identify an individual who has to consider/adhere to their religious beliefs while competing in sport.

Solutions to barriers (1)

Facilities, accessibility, equipment and transport are four areas to consider when developing solutions to participation barriers in sport.

 Facilities

Inadequate facilities for the end user can be a major barrier to participation. The issue may be the building or location itself, or how suitable (fit for purpose) it is for the given activity. For example, does the facility have suitable, safe and weather-appropriate pitches for an adults' social football league.

National research investigating the participation of women in sport found that a major barrier was a lack of changing facilities with access to hair dryers.

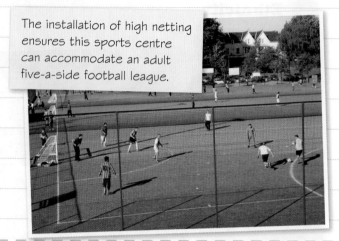

The installation of high netting ensures this sports centre can accommodate an adult five-a-side football league.

Facilities factors to consider

- ✓ Is it fit for purpose?
- ✓ Does it provide a safe environment?
- ✓ Does it comply with the Equality Act?
- ✓ Is it in a suitable location with good transport links?
- ✓ Does it have adequate changing and toilet facilities?

② **Accessibility**

Sport should be accessible for anyone regardless of their age, sex, race, ability or religion. Sports organisations are constantly being tasked to ensure their service or programme is fully inclusive and can accommodate all needs. Does it comply with the Equality Act? For example, a leisure centre will need to ensure its sessions are either designed to cater for a specific group of people (such as wheelchair basketball) or offer an inclusive environment (such as adapted indoor rowing machines to suit wheelchair users).

 Equipment

Unsafe or unsuitable equipment can be a key factor in low participation rates. Here is what James (aged 17 years) had to say after viewing his new college's fitness suite:

> I really want to join the college's gym, but I'm not impressed with the equipment. The weights area is really limited and the cardiovascular machines are really old. I don't like team sports, so do not want to join any of the sports teams, but the gym does not feel like a place I want to exercise in either.

 Transport

The location of an activity can have an impact on participation. For example, if activities take place in a rural location with poor transport links, this may limit the number of people taking part. Developers and planners always need to consider the transport links when building a new facility.

Cycle lanes are becoming increasingly popular among local councils as a way of improving transport links while being aware of the health of the community and environment.

Now try this

1 Think about **two** contrasting places or activities you have been to or taken part in where your experience has been (a) positive and (b) negative.

2 What made those experiences good and bad?

3 How could the negative experience have been improved?

Think about how external factors contributed to each experience. What were the facilities, equipment and transport like?

Solutions to barriers (2)

Staffing, staff training, financial incentives, publicity and education are more areas to consider when developing solutions to participation barriers in sport.

5 Staffing

When organising any given activity, appropriate staffing is extremely important. You will need to consider:

- staff/coach-to-participant ratio
- how to ensure appropriate staff are in place to meet the needs of participants, e.g. a female instructor for a women-only swim session
- the availability of suitably qualified/experienced staff for a particular activity/session.

6 Staff training

Instructors with inadequate training can be a potential barrier to participation, as their inability to deliver positive sessions may prevent an individual from continuing with a particular activity.

Apprenticeships are a popular method of providing new instructors with the necessary experience while undertaking a relevant qualification.

7 Concessionary rates and promotions

Income is thought to have on an impact an individual's ability to access recreational facilities. Lower socio-economic status is associated with general levels of poor health, which may affect mobility and lead to decreased levels of participation.

Facilities may use some of the following incentives to remove or decrease the financial barrier to participation.

- Discounted rates such as for off-peak usage.
- Promotions and incentives to encourage people to bring friends.
- Concessionary rates for certain groups, e.g. those on a low income, students or OAPs.

8 Publicity

The idea that a particular sport requires expensive equipment or clothing can be a barrier to participation.

The Get into Golf initiative, in partnership with Sky Sports, runs a campaign to try to overcome the perception that golf is an expensive sport. The aim of this campaign is to change people's ideas about golf and offer cheaper solutions to encourage more participation in the sport. For example, the campaign encourages people to attend low-price taster sessions at which all equipment is provided. Sessions are delivered locally by golf clubs and Professional Golf Association (PGA) professionals, enabling attendees to find out more about local golfing opportunities.

9 Education

Schools can influence participation in a positive way by providing:

- courses and training in sports leadership and officiating, potentially leading to a career in sport
- good facilities allowing young people to play sport in a safe and enjoyable environment
- extracurricular activities and club links that introduce young people to new sports and activities.

The attitude of staff can have an impact on an individual's relationship with sport and how physically active they are.

Now try this

Can you think of an activity that you have not been able to access because it is too expensive? If you were the national governing body for that sport or a club/organisation delivering that sport, what could you do to overcome this barrier?

Think about initiatives that organisations could put in place and research some examples.

Impact on community cohesion and health

The impact of sports development is measured against specific outcomes that usually have links with: community cohesion, health and well-being, regeneration, crime reduction and education.

Community cohesion   Health and well-being

Impact of sports development

Education   Regeneration

Crime reduction

Fitness classes for older people can provide a valuable sense of community while also improving health.

Community cohesion

- Sports development creates a common vision, goal and sense of belonging among individuals and communities.
- It appreciates community members' diverse backgrounds and circumstances.
- Community members benefit from similar opportunities, regardless of their background.
- Sports development promotes positive and long-lasting relationships between communities.

Strengthened by sport

- Sport allows people to come together **to share a common interest and goal**. This has a social impact as individuals get to know each other both within their own and neighbouring communities. Sport '**brings people together**'.
- People are given opportunities to **engage and become upskilled**, for instance as coaches and volunteers to run or take part in activities.

Health and well-being

There's strong evidence that taking part in sport improves health. Whatever our age, there is robust scientific evidence illustrating that being physically active can help us lead healthier lives. Regular physical activity can reduce the risk of many chronic conditions, including coronary heart disease, stroke, type 2 diabetes, cancer, obesity, and mental health problems such as depression and anxiety. There are economic benefits associated with this as any reduction in health problems means a reduction in the spending needed on the National Health Service.

Now try this

1. Identify an area near you that would benefit from more community cohesion.
2. How could you encourage this through a sports programme? What sport would you choose? Why?

Impact on regeneration, crime and education

Providing opportunities for sport can help enhance education, reduce crime and regenerate areas.

Regeneration

Regeneration is the long-term, sustainable and social, economic, physical and environmental transformation of an area that has previously been degenerated.

- Regeneration or **urban regeneration** is at the forefront of government policies.
- One way of achieving this is through hosting large sporting events, developing sports infrastructure, and the development of sporting initiatives.
- The success criteria of urban regeneration is often measured in reference to **social**, **economic**, **physical** and **environmental** regeneration.
- Sport England has identified many leisure and shared community facilities, such as parks, that need regenerating so they can create new 'community hubs'.
- Sporting facilities are built in disused areas to help **regenerate and bring economic growth** while encouraging people to use them. For example, the Olympic stadium was built in Stratford, London, to regenerate an area that was derelict.

Since the Games, some facilities built for the London 2012 Olympics are still being used and therefore bring economic profit to the area.

Crime

We know sports participation can help reduce crime, but it is important to understand how. There are three levels of crime/risk:

1 **Primary level** – personal or social circumstances may increase a person's risk of offending
- Solution – sports development initiatives to encourage community cohesion

2 **Secondary level** – people in an 'at risk' category of committing a crime
- Solution – sports development initiatives to target these people, to reduce the likelihood of them committing crime

3 **Tertiary level** – people who have already offended
- Solution – initiatives by certain agencies such as the Youth Offenders Trust, which makes referrals and places people on sports initiatives

There are different avenues for reducing crime. They are **diversion** (moving people away from a time or place they are likely to commit a crime), **deterrence** (encouraging people to stay away from crime and having harsh consequences if they don't), and **development** (developing people's skills, such as communication and teamwork).

Education

School Games is a government initiative that aims to encourage young people to take part in competitive school sport. The School Games are made up of four levels of activity: competition in schools, between schools, and at a county or national level. By providing competition in different formats it makes it more attractive and accessible for young people, and ensures they can all take part in competitive sport irrespective of their experience, talent or ability.

Schools are also responsible for developing a young person's **character** – with many now using sport as a tool to help broaden children's learning experiences and promote traits such as resilience, leadership, teamwork, respect and employability.

There is increasing evidence linking well-being and attainment in schools, with higher attaining schools having greater levels of participation in physical activity and sports programmes than lower performing schools.

Now try this

Think of other events hosted either in the UK or abroad where regenerating the area has benefited the community. In what ways has the community benefited?

Local stakeholders

Stakeholders are involved in sports development at three levels: local, national and global.
This page concentrates on the local level.

Stakeholder levels

- ✓ **Local level** involves councils and authorities, who play an important role in sports development as they are concerned with targeting different groups.
- ✓ **National level** involves government agencies such as Sport England, who are responsible for continuing to build on foundations of sporting success and increase the number of participants at all levels of the sports development continuum.
- ✓ **Global level** involves world governing bodies, such as FIFA (International Football Federation) or INF (International Netball Federation), whose primary aims are to continue to develop, promote and protect the game while encouraging more people to take up the sport.

Local authority   Facility management

> **Local sports development stakeholders**

Voluntary, public and private sectors
(can be national and global as well)

Stakeholder

A **stakeholder** is an individual, group or organisation that has a particular area of interest, such as sport.

Local authorities (LAs)

- These play a leading role in the provision and development of sport.
- They work with a range of service providers, such as health authorities and the police.
- They are concerned with the types of target groups in the community, ensuring the best opportunities for each group are accessible to them.
- They provide sport and leisure facilities to enable the community to become healthier and inclusive.
- Some LAs have sports development officers who run large-scale programmes, while others have more specific programmes, such as GP referral schemes.
- They monitor the success rate of sport and physical activity, crime rate, and so on.

Facility management

- Some sports development stakeholders at a local level are in charge of facility management.
- This involves looking after the running of the facility, which could include local leisure centres that are used for sport and physical activity.
- Both public and private stakeholders are involved.
- Stakeholders play a role in the provision and development of sport by ensuring sport and physical activity is inclusive and progressive.

Voluntary, public and private sectors

- These can be **included at local, national and global levels**; voluntary organisations are also known as 'grassroots' organisations.
- They are usually supported by volunteers who take on roles such as coaching or officiating.
- Private-sector businesses usually get involved in sports development to further their business, but also to try to give something back to the community, such as new venues and sponsorship.
- Public-sector facilities are funded both locally and nationally by grants, such as from Sport England – usually applied for via LAs.

Now try this

Imagine you are trying to set up a new community sports programme in your local area. List who your local and national stakeholders would be. Consider all of the key partners you would need to approach to make your project happen.

National- and global-level stakeholders

This page focuses on national- and global-level sports development stakeholders.

Sport England ──┐   ┌── UK Sport

┌─────────────────────────────────┐
│ **National and global stakeholders** │
└─────────────────────────────────┘

Education and ──┘   │   └── Politicians
healthcare providers   National governing bodies (NGBs)

Sport England

Sport England works alongside NGB, national partners, local government and community organisations. Sport England has three main aims:

1 To grow – it would like to see one million people taking part in sport; this includes more children taking part in five or more hours of PE and sport per week.

2 To sustain – continuing to keep people in sport and physical activity.

3 To excel – improving talent development in at least 25 sports.

UK Sport

UK Sport is responsible for promoting sport and supporting it across the UK.

UK Sport provides information on activities and initiatives being run while also helping and supporting elite athletes to compete and win medals at national and international levels, such as at the Olympics and the Paralympics. In order to do this it has two programmes:

 Podium – helps fund athletes who are close to winning medals (in under four years).

 Podium potential – helps fund those who have the potential to win medals at some point in the future.

Politicians

Government and **politicians** are important stakeholders in sports development. They tend to **raise issues** on sport and well-being at a national level. These could include issues such as potential growth for infrastructure, economic growth and health benefits.

Education and healthcare providers

The Youth Sport Trust is a national stakeholder that believes every child has a right to be physically active through quality PE and school sport. Through its partnerships with schools and practitioners, it has developed solutions to maximise the power of sport for young people. The three principal elements of its mission are well-being, leadership and achievement. The Youth Sport Trust is the leading organisation in the development of the School Games.

NHS England leads the National Health Service (NHS) in England, shares out more than £100 billion in funds, and holds organisations to account for spending this money effectively for patients and efficiently for the taxpayer. The NHS is a national sports development stakeholder as increased physical activity is linked to many health benefits.

National governing bodies (NGBs)

- These have specific aims or 'visions' for a particular sport.
- They are responsible for both the development and delivery of their sport at all levels.
- They encourage people to take up the sport through various roles such as officiating, coaching or participating.
- They are important stakeholders in continuing to develop their sport at all levels.
- Some governing bodies have **an international governing body**, such as FIFA for football. These bodies do the same job as NGBs, but on a **global scale**.

Now try this

1 Identify an NGB for a particular sport.
2 What are its main aims and objectives, and how are these achieved?

Stakeholder functions

Stakeholders have various functions such as providing funding and resources, promotion, coaching, planning, research and consultation.

Funding

A key role stakeholders can play in the organisation of sport is access to funding. Whether they can provide the funding directly, or via supporting a funding bid, stakeholders are an important aspect of partnership-working.

Resourcing

Resources help physical activity, schemes and initiatives or an event to take place. Resources can be subdivided into three categories:

1. **Human** – staff or workforce employed or volunteering to help the scheme to run.
2. **Financial** – the money and investment to enable the scheme or initiative to be successful.
3. **Physical** – tangible resources such as facilities and equipment.

Promotion

- **Promotion of a scheme or initiative** is important for stakeholders to ensure the population is aware of what is happening.
- **Mass media promotions**, such as adverts and posters, for example Sport England's 'This Girl Can' campaign, enable this to happen.

The 'This Girl Can' campaign logo

Coaching

- Stakeholders such as national governing bodies (NGBs) play an important role in providing **coaching and officiating education**.
- A variety of stakeholders or NGBs **subsidise courses to encourage** more people to enrol.
- Some NGBs focus on particular **target groups** to encourage higher participation in their coaching courses. For example, the Football Association's 'Football in the Community' scheme encourages higher participation at grassroots level.

Strategic planning

- Some sports have less private funding than others, so it is important for these 'less popular' sports to be recognised and developed.
- Strategic planning **contributes to targeting particular groups of people** to ensure they are active and have opportunities to become involved with a variety of sports and schemes.
- This is important when **funding is allocated** to ensure **the impact on development and provision is maximised**.

Research and consultation groups

- Stakeholders value **research** and often have **universities or other agencies** working on their behalf to **develop and enhance the provision** of sport and physical activity, for example the Sport England Active People Survey.
- **Consultation groups** can be included in valued research to **identify thoughts and opinions** about facilities, clubs, schemes and initiatives, for example the release of a national level consultation paper on behalf of the Department for Digital, Culture, Media and Sport.

Now try this

Imagine you want to set up a new sporting activity to increase participation among a certain target group, e.g. women or disabled people. Think of a stakeholder that can assist you in the development of the project and address how they can help you via their various functions: funding, resourcing, promotion, coaching, strategic planning and research.

Key stakeholder personnel

There are many different types of stakeholders and they all have different roles to play.

Sport-specific development officers

Community development officers

Administrators and participants — **Key stakeholders** — Community leaders

Club officials

Local authority councillors

Personnel

Personnel are people who have a particular role in an organisation.

Key stakeholder personnel

Personnel	Role
Sport-specific development officers	• Usually employed by the national governing body (NGB) to increase participation and deliver schemes and initiatives
Community development officers	• Can be employed by the NGB • Main role is to oversee and develop participation and provision in local communities • Aim to ensure targets are met
Community leaders	• Primary responsibility is for well-being and improvement of communities • May have specific responsibility for particular target groups, e.g. youth
Local authority councillors	• Responsible for approving funding for events, schemes or initiatives, e.g. Race for Life • Responsible for facilities and strategic planning
Club officials	• Usually people who are on some type of sports committee, e.g. club secretaries, treasurers • Work with other stakeholders, e.g. to ensure development of sport at different levels
Administrators	• Fulfil administrative responsibilities, e.g. keep accounts, maintain registers of members, organise logistics of travelling to or hosting league games within leagues/fixtures • Can be responsible for overall running of leagues, e.g. organising fixture schedules
Participants	• Take part in sport and physical activity

Now try this

1   Is it possible for one person to have several different roles? Explain why.
2   What do you think the advantages and disadvantages of this would be?

Purpose of measuring sports development

While agencies on a local, national and global basis have created schemes with aims and targets, it is important the schemes are planned appropriately and measured to gauge their success.

Components of sports development

	Purpose
Meeting aims	• An aim is important as it tells others what you are going to do. • Objectives explain how you are going to go about it. • The aims need to be SMART (specific, measurable, achievable, realistic and time-constrained). • This will tell us whether or not the aim has been met or not and what further improvements may need to be initiated.
Standardisation	• Standardisation refers to the standards set and whether these are being met. • Where standards are not being met this will be pointed out, and suggestions made on what may need to be improved or changed to ensure those standards are met.
Improvement	• Improvement is concerned with what may need to change to make it better.
Impact	• Impact primarily concerns how something has made a difference to an individual, community or agency, e.g. what impact has a new leisure centre had on the number of people participating in sport?

Effects on participation – increase in numbers

Inclusion and progression – more people from different target groups participating in sport

Education – raising people's awareness on the health benefits of taking part in sport and physical activity

Regeneration – money invested into areas improves facilities and community cohesion

Success measures

Crime – reduction of crime-related incidents in the local area

Community cohesion – bringing more people together from different demographics

Health and well-being – increase in health and well-being by getting more people active by using local facilities

Drug use – reduction in the use of drugs on a local and national basis, in particular where new schemes or facilities have been put in place

Now try this

1 Identify why it is important for aims of sports development to be SMART.
2 Using the internet, can you identify a local club or agency that demonstrates these targets on its website?

Methods of measuring sports development

There are several ways individual organisations can measure the success of an initiative. If initiatives and schemes are measured they are more likely to succeed, and the results can be built on.

Benchmarking ——

Quality schemes ——

Measuring sports development

Secondary research ——

Key performance indicators (KPIs)

Primary data

Benchmarking

- Benchmarking is a process where an organisation or individual, such as an LA, can **set targets and standards for themselves**. One example is Sport England setting the target of one million people taking part in one sport.
- It means that organisations can compare themselves against similar organisations or national standards.
- Benchmarking's purpose is to identify strengths and areas for improvement.
- It involves continuously **monitoring and evaluating** how targets can be reached.
- Targets should be reviewed **quarterly and annually** to check they have been met.

Quality schemes

The 'Quest' quality scheme is a way of **measuring sports development initiatives or schemes** running on a local or national basis.

- It is primarily aimed at LAs, voluntary organisations and governing bodies.
- It has been developed in partnership with Sport England.
- It is based on a percentage scoring system – the higher the percentage the better the quality considered.
- LAs, voluntary organisations and governing bodies can **assess themselves internally or be externally assessed.**

Other quality schemes include those such as Investors in People, Club Mark and the Charter Standard Scheme.

Key performance indicators (KPIs)

- KPIs are a way of **measuring or monitoring** how well a target or goal has been achieved.
- In this way, the agency or individual can identify and manage the goal or target.
- Action is taken if the target or goal is not met, through **constant monitoring and evaluation.**

KPIs will be specific to each project but could include:

- levels of participation
- the establishment of new clubs and facilities
- differences in crime rates.

Key words

Primary data is obtained **first-hand**, such as via **interviews, questionnaires and observations**. This research will aid decision-making on whether an objective or target has been reached.

Secondary research involves accessing data that has already been gathered and and published in books, online etc. This data is usually a summary of what has been collated.

Data and research

Through both primary data and secondary research, agencies such as Sport England and UK Sport are able to assess specific data that will then help them set their objectives and vision. For example, Sport England will have gathered some primary data and secondary research to create the target of one million people being involved in sport.

Now try this

1   Describe **one** advantage and **one** disadvantage of each of these measurement methods.
2   Identify **one** national or local initiative where you think one of these methods may apply.

Wider impact when hosting an event

When hosting a major sports event, there are many implications for individuals and societies. Here are five areas to consider.

1 Infrastructure

👍 Improved infrastructure can be a long-term investment, leaving a **legacy** of improved sporting venues and public transport after the event itself has finished. The London 2012 Olympics, for example, have left a lasting legacy including improved public transport.

👎 Many facilities built for events like the Olympics can never be fully used again and may be abandoned. This can be avoided by careful planning and partnership work. The London 2012 Olympic Village, for example, has been converted into affordable housing.

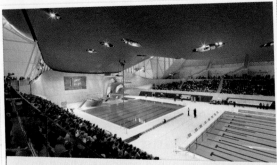

Infrastructure is the buildings, roads, communication links and facilities that are constructed for the event. The Aquatics Centre built for the London 2012 Olympics is now available to the public.

2 Political

👍 Major sporting events can raise countries' profiles and help them gain greater international acceptance. For example, when South Africa hosted the Rugby World Cup and later the Football World Cup, these were defining moments in highlighting the new 'post-apartheid' country.

👎 If the event goes badly, it can lead to negative publicity for politicians. For example, the organisers of the 2014 Sochi Winter Olympics were accused of corruption and exceeding the budget.

3 Environment

👍 Some events are developed to have minimal impact on the environment. At the London 2012 Olympics, 62 per cent of the waste was reused, recycled or composted.

👎 Large sporting events can have an ecological impact thousands of times larger than the size of the pitches/stadiums that are used, for example due to the additional infrastructure required.

4 Ethical and cultural

👍 A major sporting event can create a culture for sport, promoting participation in sport which has lasting benefits on the nation's health.

👎 Land previously used for residential or communal purposes may be built upon to create infrastructure. Shanty towns, for example, were demolished for the 2008 Beijing Olympics. This has ethical implications – should new venues be built at the cost of people's homes?

5 Economic

👍 Cities that host large events like the Olympics see an increase in tourists and business investment.

👍 An increase in investment will help create jobs and can revitalise and redevelop cities.

👎 Hosting a major sporting event like the Olympics can cost the taxpayer significant amounts of money.

👎 Costs of hosting the Olympics rise over time and can be much greater than expected.

Now try this

1 Why do you think governments have a large part to play in international events?
2 Why do you think countries think it's prestigious to host major national and international events?

 Think about the likely political concerns governments might have.

Wider impact of implementing an initiative or scheme

When implementing an initiative or scheme, there are many implications for individuals and societies. Here are five areas to consider.

1 Infrastructure

A new sports scheme or initiative can create jobs, provide facilities and redevelopment of a community.

An example of an initiative that has an impact on local infrastructure are the popular trampoline parks that are opening nationwide. They are usually found at disused warehouses in industrial areas – improving the appeal of an area, creating employment and attracting visitors.

2 Ethical/cultural/social

Sports initiatives can have a positive effect on education: improving attainment, lowering absenteeism and drop-out rates, and increasing progression to higher education.

Sports programmes can create community cohesion and contribute to keeping communities fitter and healthier.

Sports programmes aimed at young people at risk of criminal behaviour can help enhance their self-esteem and reduce reoffending. For example, the Kickz football programme has helped to reduce youth crime in north London.

3 Economic

In 2010, sport and sport-related activity contributed £20.3 billion to the English economy and supported over 400 000 full-time equivalent jobs. Implementing a sporting initiative could create new jobs or support existing ones.

Sport, as part of a wider health promotion agenda, is a good health and economic investment. For example, taking part in regular sport can save between £1750 and £6900 in healthcare costs per person (source: Sport England).

4 Political

A government's policy and priorities can have a significant impact on the sustainability of sports schemes and initiatives. For example, School Sport Partnerships were one strand of the previous Labour government's strategy; however, in October 2010, the decision was taken to end funding for School Sport Partnerships. This was controversial at the time and has been the focus of much debate since.

5 Environment and health

Participation in sport can create a significant impact on the natural environment, for example more people cycling to work can reduce pollution. It can also have a positive impact on health, creating a healthier society in which to live. Whatever our age, there is good scientific evidence that being physically active can help us lead healthier lives.

Many local authorities use the GP exercise referral scheme – GPs or other healthcare professionals will decide on a patient's eligibility based on a medical condition where an increase in exercise will benefit that patient's health. GP referral teams are usually based within a leisure centre where they will develop a 12-week programme that is tailored to an individual's lifestyle and needs.

Now try this

1 Can you identify a local initiative that benefited your community (such as free swimming for primary school children)?

2 Can you identify a national scheme or initiative that either you or someone you know has been involved in? How did it benefit you/your friend?

Think about all of the different factors listed above (infrastructure/environmental/political/ethical/cultural/economic) when researching your answer.

Wider impact of developing a facility or club

There are four main implications for individuals and societies wishing to develop facilities or clubs.

1 Infrastructure and economy

The development of new facilities can bring more jobs to an area, with regeneration putting money back into the facility so it can be updated and seen as a more 'attractive' option. An example is Tottenham Hotspur Football Club's new stadium development programme – worth over £750 million. The development will bring:

- 579 new homes
- a 180-room hotel
- a local community health centre
- 'Tottenham Experience' – a Spurs museum and club shop
- a university technical college and new club administration buildings.

2 Cultural/social/ethical

Any new development offers new opportunities, which should take into consideration the different needs of the community. These could include:

- offering subsidised access for low income groups
- disabled-friendly facilities, such as Inclusive Fitness Initiative (IFI) gyms
- family-friendly facilities
- changing and breastfeeding-friendly zones
- consideration of religious beliefs (including women-only activities)
- a dedicated room for health professionals to hold health promotion and awareness events, for example on nutrition and healthy eating, or stopping smoking

Tottenham Hotspur's Northumberland Development Project (at top of image) being built around their White Hart Lane ground.

3 Environment

- Facilities are planned to be environmentally friendly, such as being insulated to keep heat in, or built with new fabrics to ensure they are carbon-friendly.
- Many local facilities are easily accessible within the community. For example, they may be within walking distance, so less likely to require travel by car.

4 Political

- Funding may be at risk of being cut or not reallocated to the club or facility for political reasons (for example, if the controlling party wants to spend its budget elsewhere).
- Local investment in sport can be low priority compared to other initiatives from local and central government, again often because of limited budgets.

Now try this

1. Identify a facility or club in your area that needs more money to bring it up to date.
2. Why do you think stakeholders have not done this already?

Different types of media (1)

The media is now essential in sport owing to the many advantages it offers.

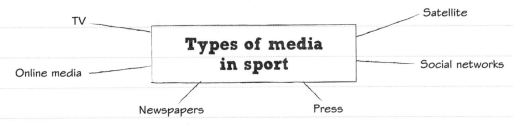

TV — Satellite

Types of media in sport

Online media — Social networks

Newspapers — Press

TV and satellite broadcasting

Role of media

- Sports-related TV programmes include **live broadcasting**, such as Sky/BT coverage of football/netball/golf.
- They also show **recorded highlights** such as Match of the Day.
- Broadcasts also include educational documentaries, the analysis of players, rules in sport and report coverage.
- They broadcast to **a large audience**, both nationally and internationally.

Effect on sports development

- TV and satellite broadcasting **promotes sport to a wide audience**, in particular new and upcoming sports, such as handball.
- Broadcasts can advertise new sporting events and major events, such as Crabbie's Grand National, Football World Cup and Wimbledon, which can bring new people to the sport.
- Viewers must sign up and pay for the rights to watch some channels, such as BT Sport/Sky Sports, which means certain events or matches are not available to everyone.
- TV and satellite broadcasting generates global interest that increases coverage, funding, sponsorship and advertising rights.

Commercialisation

Commercialisation is the way something is managed or exploited, usually in order to make a profit.

Social networks

Role of media

- Social media consists of sites such as Facebook, Twitter, Snapchat and LinkedIn.
- Social media sites can host live broadcasts about current club developments, such as players who have been signed by football clubs prior to the start of the season.
- They are advantageous as they are free, so are cost effective for the organisation.
- Some businesses that sponsor major events or clubs are linked to social networks and are advertised through other social media sites as well as their own.

Effect on sports development

- Social networks enable **promotion** of schemes, initiatives, leagues, games and sports by posting results/updates.
- They allow **fans to follow their sports teams/athletes**; for example in 2015, Barcelona Football Club had 150 million followers on social media sites and Cristiano Ronaldo was the first footballer to gain over 100 million followers on Instagram.
- Sites like Twitter can generate interest in new projects/developments through the use of hashtags.
- Social media sites can also be used in a **negative manner**, such as for writing/posting offensive or foolish updates (for example, Greek triple jumper Voula Papachristou was suspended from the national team for making a racist comment online).
- They are used for other means such as advertising and recruitment of new employees/volunteers, for example LinkedIn is used to upload online CVs to attract potential new employers.

Media coverage and involvement is essential in sport. This is because of the amount of money and exposure the media can bring.

Now try this

1. Describe **one** disadvantage of TV and satellite broadcasting and **one** disadvantage of social networks.
2. What could you do to overcome these?

Different types of media (2)

The role of the press, newspapers and online media can be advantageous or disadvantageous when covering and promoting sport.

Online media

Role of media

This can be used on a local, national and international level.

It can include websites, blogs, clips and videos, all aiming to influence the individual.

The amount of 'traffic' or users shows the owner of the online media site the number and type of people who are accessing the information.

Effect on sports development

- Websites are a good tool for promoting an event, club, scheme or facility.
- Disadvantages include being open to hacking, posting the wrong or incorrect information, or offending people.
- Videos are a popular form of online media. Having a video on a webpage can increase 'traffic' that in turn increases the number of people wanting to buy products or sell advertising rights.
- Online media is beneficial in several ways including:
  - being easily accessible
  - being easier to connect with the audience
  - being able to demonstrate an activity/facility/event
  - many people prefer to watch media such as videos than read a print article
  - people are more likely to comment on online media, thereby increasing social involvement and interest.

Press and newspapers

Role of media

- They have a duty to report the news fairly and accurately; although this is not always the case.
- There are sport-specific magazines, such as *Runner's World* for runners, that can convey specialist content.

Effect on sports development

- They can have a huge influence over how popular a sport or individual is.
- Most sports or events tend to be male biased, with reporting of male sports much greater than female or disabled sports, although this is slowly changing.
- Different newspapers have different readerships and will tailor their reporting according to what will interest their reader. This leads to sensationalist stories about athletes' personal lives in the tabloid press which can detract from the sport.
- They are important in promoting initiatives, events, clubs' and facilities' roles, giving updates and interviews.
- They can potentially increase opportunities to gain funding through different revenue streams, such as sponsorship and advertising.
- In terms of initiatives and schemes, they can help promote objectives and outcomes across into communities to generate more publicity.

The press can cover events at local, regional, national and international levels.

Now try this

1 Why do companies, teams and athletes need to be careful when it comes to reporting and using the media?
2 Which media sources, in your opinion, give you the information in the least biased manner? Why do you think this?

Use of media in sport

The media has an important role in sports development, providing coverage, reporting, advertising, promotion, a means of recruitment and funding.

Coverage and reporting

Advantages

👍 Sports coverage for national and international events, such as the Rugby World Cup or Six Nations rugby tournament, can be lucrative for the companies, teams and players involved.

👍 Local events are given 'air time' on television and radio news.

👍 Coverage promotes and advertises both the sport and the brand.

👍 Coverage could be via TV, satellite, live streaming or radio broadcasting.

👍 Coverage of large live events, such as the London Marathon, can show the excitement as it happens.

Disadvantages

👎 It can encourage looking at the athlete as opposed to focusing on their ability; for instance the Williams sisters in tennis are often criticised for the way they look rather than being assessed on their ability and achievements.

👎 It can sometimes report in a biased way or give an inaccurate account that slants the view of the reader/listener, especially in some tabloid newspapers.

👎 Reporting of local events and matches can be limited.

Advertising and promotion

Usain Bolt advertising Puma, his sponsor.

Advantages

👍 The media can promote or publicise both the sport itself and a product of some kind, for example by showing the logos of sponsors.

👍 The media can advertise directly, for example a product such as crisps, or indirectly, such as via sponsorship.

👍 It can be used to promote teams, individuals, leagues or events.

👍 Revenue is generated when high-profile athletes are shown in the media promoting their sponsors, such as Usain Bolt wearing Puma trainers to advertise the brand.

Disadvantages

👎 Bad publicity or press, such as an athlete failing a drugs test, can lead to bad press for the brand that sponsors them.

👎 Sponsors do not want to be associated with athletes or teams who have received bad publicity, so withdraw their money.

Recruiting

The media is often good at recruiting new sponsors to advertise their brands in return for promotion. For example, the Aintree Grand National was called the John Smith's Grand National and then the Crabbie's Grand National. Since 2017, the race and accompanying festival have been sponsored by Randox Health. As this is a major horse-racing event, there are three days of coverage on radio and television so the sponsors gain lots of promotion.

Funding

There are many ways the media can benefit funding:

• Increasing interest in the event or activity will increase revenue through different means, for example ticket sales, advertising, participating, sponsorship.

• This can then help with the funding of an initiative or scheme, or even a facility or club.

Now try this

What are the advantages and disadvantages of being a sports celebrity featured in the media?

Sustainable commercialisation: funding sources

Sustainable commercialisation does not aim to make as much money as possible, but rather to generate income in order to help fund a project over the long-term. There are various ways to generate income - individuals can apply for various types of funding or schemes for their club or facility. Some examples are identified here. This process usually involves writing a bid or going through an application process against criteria identifying what the money will be used for and how it will benefit the community or individuals.

Funding Central

This is a free website, accessible to charities, sports clubs and voluntary organisations, which has lots of information regarding applications for funding and finance.

JustGiving for Sports Clubs

JustGiving, Sport England and the Sport and Recreation Alliance have combined to make it easier for sports clubs **to claim gift aid**. This allows volunteers more time to participate, umpire or coach in the sport rather than deal with administration.

Torch Trophy Trust Bursary

This helps volunteers who want to undertake an officiating or coaching role but would be unable to do this without applying for this bursary.

Community Amateur Sports Club (CASC) scheme

This organisation ensures money is kept in clubs at grassroots level rather than being paid out as tax. Clubs can register for this and be exempt from tax, so in effect money goes back into their club.

> Remember there are many other funding sources that can be applied for and allocated to the community/club/individual. The ones identified here are just a small sample.

Football Foundation

The Football Foundation is a body that distributes money on a large scale to develop or improve new or existing facilities within football.

Other projects the Football Foundation approves include:

- the **'Build the Game'** scheme, which is used towards developing smaller facilities
- the **Youth Football Grant**, which is primarily geared towards community use where by clubs can access funding to buy new goalposts of different sizes
- the **Respect Equipment Scheme,** which enables organisations to receive 50 per cent off equipment costs
- the **Premier League and the FA Facilities Fund**, which provides refurbishment and development at grassroots level.

Waitrose Community Matters

Each month, every Waitrose store is given £1000 to be distributed among three local community projects. This could be anything from developing or buying new sport facilities to contributing to health charities and organisations. Other supermarkets have similar schemes.

Sport England small grants

These grants award money to projects that enable participants over the age of 14 to stay active in sport or physical activity. Sport England can award £300–£10000 towards projects initiated by non-profit organisations.

Now try this

1. Why is it beneficial for national governing bodies (NGBs) to invest heavily in facilities and community use?
2. Why do businesses such as large supermarkets become involved in awarding sports grants?

Sustainable commercialisation: budgeting

All sports clubs/facilities should budget or be able to manage their money to cover expenses such as equipment hire or maintenance. Budgets should be completed on a spreadsheet or template. Budgets must be realistic and should be completed on a regular basis. Most organisations, agencies or clubs appoint someone to do this, such as a treasurer.

	Income
Court hire	£8659
Membership fees	£5598
Sponsorship	£4000
Grants	£2500
Balance	**£20757**

Remember that the number of participants (members of a club, for example) will affect both income and expenditure.

	Expenditure
Administration costs	£6734
Hiring of officials	£3458
Court markings	£4672
Balance	**£14864**

There may also be long-term costs to consider, such as maintenance of buildings and facilities. These costs may vary from year to year.

Overall balance	**£5893**

The overall balance is the total income (£20757) minus the total expenditure (£14864).

Income and expenditure

Income is **money that is given/earned on a regular basis**, such as individuals paying subs each month for training, or paying a membership fee to use the leisure centre each month.

Expenditure is **money spent**, such as paying facility fees or league fees from a netball/tennis club.

Profit and loss

Profit is the money left after the expenditure is deducted from the income. So in the example above, the profit is £5893. If your expenditure is more than your income, you have made a **loss**. If they are the same you have **broken even**.

Record-keeping

As part of any budgetary process, accurate record-keeping is crucial. Sports clubs or organisations should always keep copies of all income and expenditure in organised files. This could include copies of receipts or proofs of purchase, and copies of invoices paid or raised. This is particularly important if an organisation has secured any external funding or grants, as accurate record keeping will form part of the conditions of the grant. If accurate records are not kept, the organisation could risk the funding being taken away from them.

Short- and long-term budgeting

Short-term budgeting means looking at your income and expenditure over the year. It is important to review this quarterly or monthly.

Long-term budgeting means looking at your income and expenditure over a number of years, typically 3–5 years. This allows you to predict or forecast changes to your budget.

Consider what may end up happening if costs escalate, and what repercussions this could have on the country.

Now try this

Complete a budget of your own income and expenditure over a set period, such as one week. Include any money you earn and what you spend it on. Is it as much as you thought? Why?

Sustainable commercialisation: distribution of funds

Sports development organisations have to be able to distribute their funds effectively across maintenance, staffing, resources and investments.

> Money needs to be spent on many things, but two major expenses for many sporting organisations are maintenance and staffing.

Maintenance

This involves the upkeep of something so it can continue to be looked after or maintained.

Large amounts of money may be needed to keep a club or facility clean, tidy or well kept. For example, people may be needed to cut grass/re-mark lines/clean changing rooms. Another example could be the checking and repair of equipment.

At times maintenance can be **expensive** but it is necessary to guarantee the continued use of equipment and facilities.

Staffing

Staffing involves the hiring, selection, training and overseeing of individuals to deliver a particular job. It is often associated with responsibilities and targets that are reviewed to ensure people are doing the jobs they are paid to do.

Staffing can either be **voluntary** (in which case individuals do not get paid) or **employed**. It is important the right number of staff is available to run the scheme, club or facility. When people refer to the term 'understaffed' it means there are not enough people to help with the task in hand. This sometimes leads to people being overstretched and doing jobs that they may not be trained to do. If a job is not completed properly, this will have an impact on the efficiency of the organisation.

Resources

Typically, resources are **materials, staffing, energy, finance, ideas or knowledge** that benefit a person or an organisation. For example, a resource for the Rio 2016 Olympics was voluntary staff, who helped give people directions to and from the venues, or helped look after athletes' clothing when they were involved in the track events in athletics.

> Resources such as team kit and equipment need to be budgeted for.

Investment

An investment is **committing** something (usually money) to gain a return.

For example, repairs may need to be made to a facility to ensure people can continue to use the equipment, so you need the money to invest in those repairs. You may also have money invested to help with the success of a club. For example, a Sunday league netball club may decide to pay for their own players to complete an officiating qualification. This is advantageous to the club as it means that they won't have to pay or find external umpires to officiate their games.

Now try this

Why is it important for agencies, facilities or clubs to keep an eye on their expenditure?

Ethics of commercialisation

The ethics of commercialisation involves balancing the benefits of private financial and commercial investment in sport with ethical considerations.

Ethics

Ethics are morals that define a person's or organisation's behaviour or activity.

Ethics in commercialisation is associated with the commercial behaviours or actions of an agency, body or business, or of someone representing them.

Commercialisation

Commercialisation is the way something is managed or exploited, usually in order to make a profit.

Arsenal have been associated with Emirates since 2004. The deal, which includes naming rights to the Emirates Stadium as well as shirt sponsorship, is one of the biggest in football in terms of revenue earned.

Ethics of commercialisation

There are many examples of sports organisations, such as football clubs, conducting themselves in an unethical way.

For instance, in February 2016, Liverpool football fans made a stand when it was announced that ticket prices for home games would rise to £77 a seat, which many long-time fans could not afford. They felt this was unethical because the club was exploiting their loyalty. In protest, fans walked out of the grounds in the 77th minute. As a result, Liverpool Football Club agreed not to raise ticket prices.

In 2016 Liverpool fans succeeded in persuading the club not to raise ticket prices.

Appropriate sponsorship and funding

The sponsorship of sport by fast food and sugary drinks companies, has been accused of being inappropriate because their products are considered to be unhealthy. Concerns have been raised about these brands being promoted to those people (particularly to children) who watch major sporting events such as the Commonwealth or Olympic Games. Tobacco advertising is no longer allowed in many sports for similar reasons.

One of the government's key agendas is to ensure private financial gain and commercialisation in sport is balanced so that mixed messages are not portrayed or promoted.

Fairtrade resourcing

- Organisations such as the Fairtrade Foundation and Fairtrade International work to ensure Fairtrade is promoted throughout the world.
- They have four key areas of focus: independent certifying and licensing of products, aiding growth and demand to empower sellers such as farmers, working alongside partners to produce goods, and raising awareness of both the Fairtrade Foundation and Fairtrade International trademarks.
- Some sporting organisations embrace this by sourcing Fairtrade material, refreshments or kit.

Now try this

1. Name some other companies whose sponsorship of national or global events might be deemed as controversial.
2. Why do you think these companies choose to sponsor these events? Do they gain anything other than financially?

Impact of the media and commercialisation

The media and commercialisation of sport can actually influence the way in which a club, event or sport is run. Here are some examples.

Impact on popularity and participation

Media coverage of sport is widespread and can be found in many forms. Participation in sports covered by the media is always higher than for those that are not.

Every summer, various initiatives capitalise on increased interest in tennis as a result of the 'Wimbledon effect' (the influence of televising the famous tournament).

An example is Liverpool City Council's 'Tennis for free' initiative, which offers free tennis sessions in its parks to encourage maximum uptake while it is also being promoted through the media and television.

Impact on progression

Timings

The start of major football matches may be timed to maximise the audience and, therefore, their exposure to advertising. Half-time of televised sports may also be extended for the same reason. Later matches may be at the expense of tired players.

Funding

The development of a new facility can be dependent on corporate sponsorship. For example, Allianz's £8 million sponsorship of the Saracens helped the club to offset the cost of redeveloping their stadium, known as Allianz Park. In 2017 they were granted permission to build a new £20 million stand.

Accessibility

Many viewers watch sports on their computers or mobile devices. British Table Tennis streams matches live on Facebook. This makes viewing sports more accessible to fans and they may be inspired to participate.

Impact on inclusion and diversity

Nicola Adams, the first woman to win an Olympic boxing title, uses the media not only to raise awareness of women's boxing but also the pay gap between male and female boxers.

Despite the prominence of male sports, the economic power of women is increasingly recognised by both the media and brands. Women's football is increasingly popular and is now broadcast across the world. Some sponsors also focus on diversity by showing support for gay and transgender athletes, such as Guinness's videos about rugby player Gareth Thomas.

Impact on rules and regulations

As a result of being broadcast, many sports have had rule changes to reduce complexity, speed up the game or make it more exciting. For example:

- the 'golden goal' rule in football keeps viewers watching to the end
- badminton's rules were changed in 2006 to regulate the length of games and to keep viewers' attention.

These types of changes can also make organising competitions easier as matches are more likely to keep on schedule.

The media's goal-line technology, or ability to record accurately the first toe over the finish line, can affect the outcome of games or races.

Twenty20 cricket is an example of an entire competition structure that was developed to increase the commercial appeal of a sport.

Now try this

Can you think of any examples in which the media has played a part in influencing your engagement or participation in a particular sport or activity?

Proposal writing

Sports development proposals may be for an event, initiative, scheme, or the development of a facility or club. Before they write a proposal, there are several areas that organisations or individuals need to consider.

Why write a sports development proposal?

A **proposal** is a type of plan or suggestion. The idea of a sports development proposal is to set out:

☑ what the organisation wants to achieve

☑ how they are going to do it.

It also highlights the resources, such as people, funding and timeframe (for example, one, two, three years or longer) that the organisation and individuals will be working towards.

The rationale

There has always got to be a reason for a sports development proposal. For example, Orford Jubilee Park in Orford, Warrington, is a large sports complex built to develop a flagship sports complex. The rationale was that previously there were few facilities and little community leisure use in the area. This project was built on an old landfill site and was funded by over 20 different organisations from the public, private and the voluntary sectors. It had been in planning for 15 years. The level of support contributed to the rationale.

Research

Research is important as the organisation will need to provide knowledge and evidence for why the initiative or scheme will be needed. This is important to gain resources such as funding, and to entice potential partners such as LAs, national governing bodies and sometimes national organisations to back the scheme. Other areas of research, for example for the planning of a new facility replacing an old leisure centre, would be the potential number of customers, repair costs and likely level of maintenance.

Targeted aims

Organisations must create a number of relevant targeted aims that will help achieve the overall objective of the sports development plan. Things to consider are:

- What do you want to achieve?
- What resources do you need to achieve it?
- How will you measure its impact – how will you know if it is a success or not?
- Are the aims specific to the overall objective?

Research sources

In order to identify correctly what needs to be done, both general and specific research need to be carried out. The data should cover past, present and future, which may strengthen the proposal of the development plan. For example:

- What are the current trends or ongoing related projects (for example, are similar schemes in similar areas a success)? If so, why?
- How can you interpret current data from different agencies? For example, how do you know that your proposed project will still be successful in five years' time?
- What evidence have you used to back up your assumptions and estimates?

Remember: the more research and evidence you have, the more it will strengthen the proposal.

Now try this

Think of a scheme that may benefit your area. What evidence and research is available to strengthen your case that there is a need for it in your community?

Proposal structure

Whether a proposal is for the development of an event, facility, initiative, scheme or club, it should have a clear structure with relevant headings.

What the structure should include

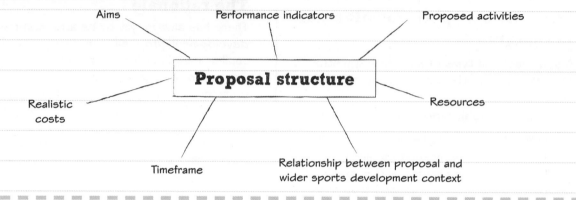

Aims

This is a statement of what the organisation wants to achieve. The aims should be based upon research, while demonstrating inclusivity by seeking to increase participation from different groups (such as women, ethnic groups or disability groups).

It is very important that the organisation shows how the proposed development plan links in, or 'fits', with the reasons why it is needed and its intended outcomes. This should be evidenced from the research carried out prior to producing the development plan proposal.

Performance indicators

- Organisations **need to measure** how successfully they have met their aims. As the project progresses, they also need to **continue to evaluate** where they started, where they want to be and how to get there.
- The criteria chosen will be used to determine whether the project has been successful.
- For example, performance indicators could include participation rates from target groups, the establishment of new clubs and facilities, or the analysis of differences in crime rates.
- It is important that there is a definitive link between the performance indicators and the aims. For instance, in order to measure whether more disabled people are taking part in an activity or event, participant numbers must be recorded, for example in a register.

Proposed activities

- Any proposed activity needs to fulfill a particular need.
- You need to have research to show evidence of the need.
- The activities selected should be clearly linked to the proven need. Types of activity include promotion, participation events (such as free taster sessions), promotional events (such as charity nights), or events focused on health and well-being.
- Some events 'tick' more than one box (for example, a charity cycle ride that focuses on health and well-being as well as raising money for a good cause).
- Remember to take into account the technical competence (skills and knowledge) of those who may be running the activities, and the event logistics (what needs to be done for it to happen).

Now try this

1. Think of a facility or club in your local area you would like to develop. How can you make this more beneficial for the community? What are your ideas or aims?
2. What evidence do you have to prove your ideas would enhance the club or facility?

Timeframe, costs and resources

It is important to include details of realistic timeframes, costs and resources in your proposal.

Timeframe

- It is important for an organisation to plan an appropriate timeframe within which to meet their target/achieve their aims.
- It is also important to be realistic when setting this timeframe. For instance, you would not be able to measure the impact of increased long-term participation within the first two months of the facility's operation.
- What may be measured within two months of opening, for example, is whether individuals from certain target groups (such as the over-50s) are using the facility.
- It might therefore be appropriate to take measurements at suitable intervals within the overall timeframe.

Key definitions

Timeframe concerns the amount of time you have to complete or achieve your aims.

Resources are the materials, money, staff and other assets needed by the organisation in order to run efficiently or effectively.

Realistic means having a sensible and practical idea of what is happening, and knowing that it can be achieved or is expected.

Realistic costs

Conducting detailed research is important when investigating costs. It is also important to explore different streams of funding and to negotiate costs so a balance is struck between realistic costs and value for money.

- If estimated costs are too low, funders may not believe your figures and you may not receive the money you want to fund the project.
- If you estimate or bid for more money than is realistic, funders may not feel they are getting value for money and declineto support the proposal.

It is therefore important that all costs are calculated and budgeted.

Factors to incorporate when budgeting include logistical costs as well as human resources costs, such as qualified coaches and other staff (for example maintenance staff.).

As an example, below are some costs for after-school sports coaching sessions. The sessions will run every Wednesday after school (3.30–4.30pm) for two six-week blocks.

Coaching cost per hour	£35
Facilities cost per hour	£40
Number of hours	12
Total coaching cost	£420
Total facilities cost	£480
Total cost	£900

Types of resource

Resources can be grouped under three headings.

- **Human** – These are the people who are required to meet the objectives and aims of the project. This can include cleaning, maintenance and administration staff as well as coaches and officials. They must have the appropriate technical competence to fulfil their roles.
- **Financial** – This is the investment or money needed to meet the aims of the plan. This could be sourced from local and/or national partners on a public, private or voluntary basis.
- **Physical** – These are facilities, materials and equipment needed to meet the plan.

Without the organisation considering each of these areas, and how they link together in the form of logistics, the proposed sports development plan is likely to fail.

Now try this

Why is it important for organisers of international events such as the Olympics or Paralympics to keep an eye on their costs?

Consider what may end up happening if costs escalate, and what repercussions this could have on the country.

Interrelationship between proposals and the wider context

When writing your proposal, you should consider how it could influence the wider sports development context, and how the wider context could impact your proposal. You need to consider all the factors discussed in this unit, including: ways of enabling participation, inclusivity and progression; infrastructure and environmental, political, ethical, cultural and economic influences; and the effect of commercialisation and the media. This page identifies key areas to consider for an example scenario.

Basketball Boost

A Birmingham housing estate has seen an increase in antisocial behaviour, with residents complaining about disruption caused by a group of young people. The police have unsuccessfully tried to engage with the youths, but youth workers have found they are interested in basketball.

PROPOSAL PLAN
Aim

To provide positive sporting activities in a disadvantaged area to bring about social cohesion and reduce antisocial behaviour through a social basketball league.

Performance indicators

- Number of young people attending the weekly sessions.
- Reduction in antisocial behaviour.
- Number of young people transitioning into basketball club sessions.
- Number of volunteers recruited to assist at sessions.

Proposed activities

To set up a social basketball league every Friday evening for young people.

Resources available

- Outside basketball court and portable net within estate grounds on the multi-use games area; access to the community centre in bad weather.
- Coaches/Volunteers – links to local basketball club.
- Marketing material/administrative assistance.

- Increased participation in sport/physical activity, contributing to healthier lifestyles in the community
- More social cohesion due to inclusivity, improving the well-being and happiness of residents
- Less antisocial behaviour, reducing the risk of crime
- Development of workforce, for example volunteers can develop life/employment skills

Stakeholders for proposal

Housing association   Sports development officer

Police

Friday night basketball

Youth players

Schools   Youth workers

Residents   Local authority   Basketball club

Commercialisation of programme

This proposal could make a significant difference and contribution to society. Potential sponsors and funders could be:

- Basketball national governing body
- Sport England
- Local authority
- Private businesses who want to engage with the community
- Housing association
- Police
- Local MPs and councillors

Use of media

Social media is an effective method of communicating and promoting activities to a target audience, especially of young people. It is usually free and, used in conjunction with other methods, can be extremely powerful.

Now try this

Imagine this is your proposal and you need to attract investment in the project to make it happen. How will you convince the various stakeholders to 'buy into' the project?

Think about what each stakeholder will gain from being involved.

Your Unit 19 set task

Unit 19 will be assessed through a task, which will be set by Pearson. In this assessed task you will need to show your ability to plan and develop a sports proposal for a given scenario.

Revising your skills

Your assessed task could cover any of the essential content in the unit. You can revise the unit content in this Revision Guide. This skills section is designed to **revise the skills** you might need for your assessed task. The section uses selected content and outcomes to provide an example of ways to apply your skills.

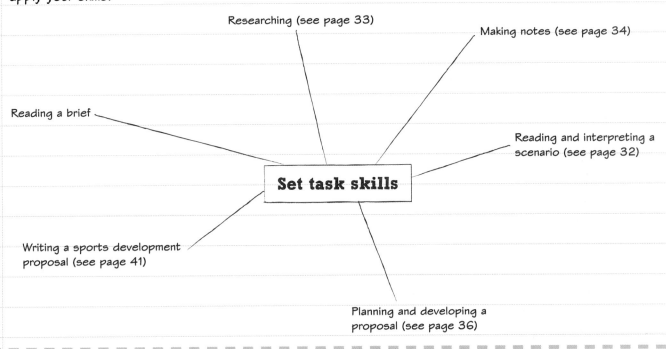

Researching (see page 33)

Making notes (see page 34)

Reading a brief

Reading and interpreting a scenario (see page 32)

Set task skills

Writing a sports development proposal (see page 41)

Planning and developing a proposal (see page 36)

Workflow

The process of writing a sports development proposal might follow these steps:

- ✓ Read a brief, carry out appropriate research and make notes.
- ✓ Revise topics relevant to the task.
- ✓ Read a scenario carefully.
- ✓ Plan a proposal.
- ✓ Create a sports development proposal using specified sections.

Check the Pearson website

The activities and sample response extracts in this section are provided to help you to revise content and skills. Ask your tutor or check the Pearson website for the most up-to-date **Sample Assessment Material** and **Mark Scheme** to get an indication of the structure of your actual assessed task and what this requires of you. The details of the actual assessed task may change so always make sure you are up to date.

Now try this

Visit the Pearson website and find the page containing the course materials for BTEC National Extended Diploma in Sport. Download the latest Unit 19 Sample Assessment Material and make a note of:

- the structure of your set task, and whether it is divided into parts
- how much time you are allowed for the task, or different parts of the task
- what briefing or stimulus material will be provided
- any notes you might have to make and whether you are allowed to take selected notes into your supervised assessment
- the activities you are required to complete and how to format your responses.

Task information and research sources

Here are some examples of skills involved in reading a task brief and scenario, and then gathering effective and relevant information to plan and develop a sports proposal.

Task

Carry out research into the development and provision of sport and physical activity, based on the scenario below.

Scenario

You are on the committee for Vulchers Netball Club, which is an amateur club in the north-west of England.

You should consider:

- Principles of Sports Development
- Wider Sports Development Concepts
- Media and Commercialisation in Sport
- Proposal Writing for Sport Development (for an event, initiative or facility development).

Responding to task information

This scenario is used as an example to show the skills you need for your assessment. The content of the scenario will be different each year and the format may also be different.

Your research needs to be recent as well as relevant to the scenario.

You might want to look into events that similar netball clubs have run, initiatives they have set up or facilities or clubs they have developed. These might be local to you, or be small clubs elsewhere.

It's a good idea to research the aims of national stakeholders for netball as well.

Sources of research

Research sources might include:

✓ articles related to the information given (e.g. online newspapers)

✓ council websites, to examine local case studies

✓ wider sports development agencies, such as Sport England or England Netball, to examine how they may have created something similar

✓ interviews/meetings with local sport development officers for ideas that may be generic or specific to the sport.

Example research

This is an example of an extract from a relevant source when considering the principles of sports development for netball.

Walking Netball is an inclusive initiative aimed particularly at older participants or those with injuries or low fitness levels.

Clear data from sports development stakeholders show an increase in participation, reaching a peak.

> Sport England has revealed that over 180 000 people aged over 16 play netball at least once a week (England Netball, 2016). This is the highest figure since the Active People Survey was launched ten years ago. In 2016, 25 400 more people were playing netball than in 2015, which is an increase of 16.4% (England Netball, 2016). This may be due to campaigns such as 'Walking Netball' and 'Back to Netball'. 'Walking Netball' is a slower version of the game, designed so people of any age or fitness level can participate. As well as the health benefits it offers, many participants enjoy the social aspect of meeting up with people in their community.

This initiative has positive impacts on community cohesion and health.

Annotate your research, referring back to the scenario. In this case the learner has identified evidence of participation and the impact of initiatives on the wider community.

Now try this

Research England Hockey's 'Back to Hockey' scheme on its website and compare it to the 'Back to Netball' scheme.

- List at least **two** similarities.
- List at least **two** differences.

Reading and interpreting research

When reading sources, you need to identify key points that might be useful in a proposal. Below are two example sources found by a student who was given the task and scenario on page 32. The first is from a local newspaper and the second is from a council website. Read the notes the student has made about these sources to help you understand how to interpret your own research.

Lincoln Lions five-a-side tournament

The Lincoln Lions women's football club, in partnership with their local sports development officer, hosted a five-a-side football tournament to attract and generate new younger players (14+ years) to their club and new 3G pitch. Their sponsors, EAL and Football Pitches Limited, generated awareness via online advertising, and poster and flyer deposits at local libraries, shops and schools.

As a result of the event, several new and existing adult members now regularly attend coaching and refereeing courses. Lincoln's women's football development officer said: 'The tournament, which attracted 60 new players, was a raging success in building this club'.

Forty-five new players have enrolled for the next season, making Lincoln Lions one of the biggest women's football clubs in the area.

The aim of this tournament was to attract and generate new younger players (the target group).

A physical resource, the new 3G pitch, could have contributed to the increase in players.

EAL and Football Pitches Limited were the national stakeholders.

A variety of targeted media was used to generate awareness.

The tournament resulted in an increase in coaching and refereeing staff, expanding the club's human resources.

Although 60 new players have signed up it's not clear whether these are younger players, so the event may not have fully achieved its aim.

Identify the key points in the research which you will also have to consider your proposal. In this case the learner has identified the aim, stakeholders, use of media and whether the activity met the aim.

'Back to' schemes are popular ways of attracting adult participants back into a sport or activity they may have played as a child or young adult.

The number of participants increased steadily in the first months with a drop-off in December which could be due to the Christmas break. The participation rate increased in January and February.

The programme has had a positive impact on participation, seeing more women playing netball and 10 participants transitioning into the main club sessions.

Key term

Throughput: This is the term used to determine attendance figures over a certain time period.

'Back to Netball' Club Participation Report

An amateur netball club has set up an England Netball initiative to increase participation in netball at their club among women aged 16+. The report lists the participation figures since the introduction of the programme six months ago.

Month	No. of unique participants	Throughput (based on one session per week × 4 weeks)
September	5	20
October	15	60
November	30	120
December	10	40
January	30	120
February	40	160

Number of participants who have transitioned into main club sessions and become a member of the club: **10**

Analyse any facts and figures in your research to help inform your own proposal.

Now try this

How have the two projects on this page contributed to the wider sports development agenda? What has been the wider impact?

Consider the wider benefits of sport and participation in sport, such as physical and health benefits.

Making notes

To help you develop your proposal, you need to make clear notes on the research you carry out.

Focus your notes

👍 Use bullet points.

👍 Make sure your notes are relevant to the task.

👍 Include key facts and figures from your research.

👎 Don't write multiple pages of notes.

👎 Don't copy large chunks of information from your research.

Making preparatory notes

You may be allowed to take some of your preparatory notes into your supervised assessment time. If so, there may be restrictions on the length and type of notes that are allowed. Check with your tutor or look at the most up-to-date Sample Assessment Material on the Pearson website for information.

Sample notes extract

- Activity = Lincoln Lions Women's FC hosted a 5-a-side football tournament.
- Aim = attract and generate new younger players (14+ years).
- Stakeholders = EAL and Football Pitches Limited were sponsors.
- Outcome = new and existing adult members attending coaching and refereeing courses – not just increased rates of performers, these roles are important if the club is to grow further.
- 60 new players – good result for amateur club such as that in the scenario.
- 45 new players enrolled for the next season.
- Lincoln Lions one of the biggest women's football clubs in the area.

Note-taking can be in shorthand, e.g. use FC instead of Football Club.

Keep in mind the specific requirements of the scenario, to ensure your notes are relevant, in this case to an amateur women's netball club in the north-west of England. Although this extract covers a football event, many of the principles can apply to netball participation schemes.

Consider the impact on different roles such as coaches, referees and volunteers, not just performers!

Facts and figures are an effective way of providing supporting evidence.

Sample notes extract

Always state the source of your information. It can be presented in brackets.

Your research should always relate back to any scenario or other information you have been given. In this case, the scenario focuses on a local women's netball club.

- 'Back to Netball' and 'Walking Netball' – participation projects.
- 180 000 people aged 16+ playing netball at least once a week (Active People Survey, Sport England, 2016).
- Participation increased by 16.4% between 2015 and 2016.
- 25 400 playing nationally.
- Locally, 10 new regular participants is a good outcome.

Now try this

Make notes on England Hockey's 'Back to Hockey' scheme from the information on its website. Use the tips listed above. Consider the following in particular:

- What is the aim of the scheme?
- What are some of the wider impacts listed?

Reviewing further information

If you need to review further information, make sure you read and analyse it carefully. Look at the example task and detailed scenario below, which expands on the brief scenario from page 32.

Task

You are required to create a proposal and analyse the interrelationship between your proposal and the wider sports development context.

The proposal must be for an event.

Use your research into the given scenario and the development and provision of sport and physical activity. The proposal should be structured as follows:

- Aims
- Performance Indicators
- Proposed Activities
- Resources.

This example task is for an event but you must also be prepared to write a proposal for something else, such as an initiative, facility or development.

Make sure you reference your research throughout your proposal.

You must explain how the aims of your proposal meet a need demonstrated in the scenario.

Your performance indicators should explain how you will measure your aims.

If a structure is supplied like this, make sure you use it rather than thinking of your own.

Read the scenario several times so that you are familiar with it. Underline the key facts to focus your thinking.

Scenario

You are on the committee for Vulchers Netball Club, which is an <u>amateur club</u> in the north-west of England. You have slowly grown the club since 2010 and now have <u>four adult teams</u>, <u>two junior teams and one junior development squad</u>. All teams play at the weekend with one team also playing in a local league on a Wednesday night. The whole club trains on a Tuesday. In total, <u>60 girls and women</u> train. The local population is approximately 16 000 and there are several netball clubs in your area. You would like to continue to grow the club and would like to create an adult 'Back to Netball' section that will represent your club.

In the winter you train in a school sports hall. In the summer you train outdoors as it is cheaper to rent the courts, <u>but two out of four courts are in poor condition</u>. Each member of your club pays <u>£18 per month for membership and £2 per game</u>. You are a very sociable club but would like to <u>host more fundraisers</u> to build up your funds. You know there is scope to extend the adult membership of the club as you were recently involved in a city sport promotional event, at which you were inundated with <u>enquiries about getting back to netball</u>.

The size of the local population could feed into your performance indicators section.

Establish the rationale/reason for developing a new project. This will provide the aim. Here, the club has been slowly growing and the aim is to increase participation through an adult 'Back to Netball' section.

Consider whether the aims of the 'Back to Netball' programme match those of the Vulchers Netball Club.

It seems as though the club is restricted by its facilities. Before developing any new project, you will need to establish whether the club has the capacity to take on new participants.

Now try this

Explain how the club's facilities could limit the club's ability to deliver the programme successfully. What could the club do to overcome these potential barriers?

Planning a proposal

It is important to plan a logical and well-written proposal before you start writing.

Sample notes extract

Proposed event Social netball league

Aims

1. To increase the number of women playing netball by developing a 'Simple Seven' social netball league, consisting of six teams of ten players.

2. To increase the number of participants becoming members.

3. To retain at least 10 new participants for the league next summer.

Performance indicators

- Register of new players and reserve list.

- Number of league players: six teams of ten players, playing competitively once a week for 6 weeks = 60 unique participants, 360 throughput attendance.

- 20% of participants signing up as members/ transitioning into main club sessions = 10–12 new participants.

Proposed activities

- To host and organise a six-week social netball league.

Resources

- Physical: courts, equipment.

- Human: umpires and timekeepers, administrators.

- Financial: promotional material, venue hire (external funding needed?)

If you write your plan in **bullet or numbered form**, you can include more information and stick to the most important points.

The three aims here complement each other. Everything in your proposal needs to relate back to your aims so it's essential that these are clear.

Include a timeframe and specific figures in your aims.

Make sure that your performance indicators are **measurable**. Here the indicators are measured by an attendance register.

Try to be specific when talking about the resources needed for your proposal. You will need to show that you have thought about **physical**, **human** and **financial** resources.

Think about how the project can help meet wider sports development outcomes, such as those of Sport England.

Consider how the proposal improves physical well-being.

Think about how the proposal affects participants' well-being, for example by increasing self-confidence, delivering educational or employment benefits, and bringing communities together.

Sample notes extract

Interrelationship between the proposal and wider sports development

- Sport England's 'Sporting Futures' outcomes.

- Sport England's 'This Girl Can' campaign.

- Increase the % of women playing/participating in sport/ physical activity.

- Increase the fitness level of women – helping to reduce health problems.

- Improve well-being of women through involvement in a social activity – making new friends, community cohesion.

Now try this

Think about how you could implement a 'Back to Hockey' scheme at your local hockey club. Use the example of the proposal plan above to make a short plan for the following aspects of your scheme: Aims, Performance indicators, Proposed activities, Resources and Interrelationship to sport development.

Writing about aims

When identifying and providing a rationale for the aims of a proposal, you must be clear and specific to show your knowledge and understanding of sports development. Justify the aims to show they are relevant to the scenario by applying and referencing relevant current research.

Sample response extract

In the south-west of England, reportedly 3500 participants play in some sort of amateur netball club or participate in a 'Back to Netball' league. However, in the northwest, where Vulchers is based, a number (580) of participants would like to take part but are unable to, owing to lack of opportunities and facilities (Sport England website; www.sportengland.org). We would like to increase netball participation in north-west England by giving individuals in this area the opportunity to join a team or enter as a team/group of friends to play some social, or even competitive, netball.

 Providing figures from relevant research can help provide background to the proposal.

 Where possible, reference your research.

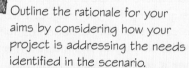 Outline the rationale for your aims by considering how your project is addressing the needs identified in the scenario.

Sample response extract

Using numbered bullet points is a clear way of displaying your aims.

Use one clear, concise, short paragraph per aim.

As a club, we would like to increase both participation and activity in this sector by running a six-week league for six teams. The overall aims are:

1. To organise and host a six-week league with six teams of ten players, playing at various times across the allocated evenings.

2. To increase the number of women playing netball by representing the club or playing in a weekly organised event that will promote the club.

3. To retain around 10 of these 'Back to Netball' participants by next summer, ideally to represent the club at the 'Back to Netball' level through the 'Simple Seven' midweek league. Retaining 10 new participants would grow the club by around 16 per cent, which is how much national participation has increased between 2015 and 2016 (England Netball).

Providing figures will support your performance indicators.

Providing a timeframe as part of the aim can contribute to of your performance indicators.

Link your aims to current research.

Remember to keep the aims clear and concise.

Now try this

Write out in more detail the aims for your 'Back to Hockey' initiative. Include relevant research from their website or other national governing bodies to support each aim.

 Consider including facts and figures.

Writing about performance indicators

When identifying relevant performance indicators, you should link them to the aims of the proposal and to the scenario, applying and referencing your research where possible.

Sample response extract

Ensure your performance indicators relate to the specific aim.

Performance indicators for aim 1

'To increase the number of women playing netball by developing a 'Simple Seven' social netball league, consisting of six teams of ten players.'

I would ensure I kept a register of any players or teams who have signed up for the league. I would also keep a reserve list, in case the league becomes full but some individuals would like to play in the future. The register will detail whether a player is male or female.

In addition, I would record the number of people, if any, who already attend Vulchers training sessions but would fit better into this sector of the group (for example, the less able).

Performance indicators should detail how you will show that your aims have been achieved.

Registers are an effective way of benchmarking the standard you want to meet.

Participants would need to complete a participation consent form. This can provide you with information on their gender, ethnicity, age or disabilities to ensure you are providing inclusive opportunities.

Consider the numbers you set in your aims (i.e. 6 weeks × 6 teams × 10 players) and use your performance indicators to address whether these have been met.

Weekly attendance registers are necessary to track participation trends – they also provide you with key evidence.

Sample response extract

Performance indicators for aim 2

'To increase the number of participants becoming members.'

My biggest indicator would be the number of teams (6) and women (60) who turned up each week to play in the league. By keeping a weekly register, I would be able to identify who is most likely to stay and play in the league. This would be my primary evidence to show/prove to other agencies (such as the netball sports development officer) the popularity of, and lack of opportunities in the area for, this type of activity. I would analyse the figures to see if any new players were recruited into different teams.

Sample response extract

Performance indicators for aim 3

'To retain at least 10 new participants for league next summer.'

I would measure the number of participants we gained from the league who were still playing by the start of the 'Simple Seven' league the following summer. Ten new participants would grow the club by around 16%, matching the 2015–2016 national increase (England Netball).

I would continue to recruit, and measure the number of, women who were on the reserve lists, who wanted to play or train but not in a competitive environment.

Link your performance indicators back to your research wherever possible.

You may want to think about retaining the participants beyond the summer league to bring about a change in behaviour – creating healthier lifestyle choices and lifelong participation.

Remember, this is how you are going to demonstrate impact.

Now try this

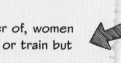

Include details from your research into the 'Back to Hockey' scheme.

Write performance indicators for the local 'Back to Hockey' initiative. You could create at least two performance indicators that link to each of the aims you identified on page 36.

Writing about activities

When proposing activities, you must relate them back to the scenario, aims and relevant research evidence. Remember to justify the proposed activities, showing their relevance to the scenario, to include realistic timeframes and to show your knowledge of sports development.

Sample response extract

My proposed activity is to organise and host a 'Back to Netball' league for women, with the aim of increasing the number of women playing netball by developing a 'Simple Seven' social netball league. It is important for the league to be fun, as the aim is mainly to increase social participation, but there also needs to be the opportunity to develop skills and knowledge in order to maintain the competitive element.

Current data shows that nationally 180 000 people aged 16+ are playing netball at least once a week (Active People Survey, Sport England, 2016), with 'Walking Netball' and 'Back to Netball' seeing an increase in participation by 16.4% (Netball England, 2016). To retain participants there must be opportunities for clubs, facilities and events so they continue to run and develop.

> In this 'activities' section you should include detail about what you are going to do to achieve your aims.

> Remember to demonstrate the rationale or reason behind the proposal – why are you doing it?

> Include research to support your reasoning – this can be national and/or local.

> Consider the 5 Ws: Who/What/ Why/ Where/When. This example describes **what** the event is and **why** the evidence suggests it might meet the aims.

> Think about who is going to help you make the event happen – which partners will you use?

Sample response extract

- The event will be supported by club officials and administrators, such as timekeepers and money collectors.
- The event will run at the local school sports hall every Thursday, starting at 7pm, with the last game being played at 8.30pm. The event will run over six weeks.
- The club will not make a profit on this league and all income will be spent on expenses, such as court hire, umpire and administration costs, medals and trophies.
- Promotional flyers and posters will be printed on coloured paper or using coloured inks, as England Netball (2013) claims that, if marketing is bright, fun and colourful, more people will be attracted to and interested in reading about events.

> Include a realistic timeframe which will give you enough time to meet your aims.

> Remember the 5 Ws. This example describes **who** (club officials and administrators), **where** (sports hall) and **when** (times), as well as **how** the event will be promoted.

> Reference relevant research where possible.

> Make sure you include the 5 Ws: Who/What/Why/Where/When.

Now try this

Thinking back to your own proposal's aims and performance indicators, jot down an idea for your proposed activity for your 'Back to Hockey' scheme. The activity should link back to your aims. Make sure you include at least four details about your activity.

Writing about resources

When considering the resources needed to meet the aims, ensure they are realistic, linked to relevant research, and justified in the context of the activities.

Sample response extract

Physical and human resources

Courts

At the school, outdoor courts with posts are available and are seldom used in the summer, so I will use these. However, two out of four courts are in poor condition, which will mean either limiting play to two courts (which will reduce the number of participants) or finding more funding to improve the courts.

Equipment

The equipment will be borrowed from Vulchers Netball Club, including four sets of bibs and three balls.

Human resources

Several people from the club will be needed to organise and run the event, e.g. volunteers to umpire and time-keep, manage the administration registers and answer phone calls, etc, as well as to deliver and promote the event via websites and the free local newspaper. Many of these roles can be filled by volunteers, but we will set aside a fee for an hour of paid time per week.

> Consider all the physical resources you will need to make your proposal happen – do they have a cost implication?

> Consider any equipment you could borrow or use for free.

> Think about the people needed to make it happen, from start to finish.

Sample response extract

Financial resources

In order to host and run the six-week league, the following costs have been calculated (figures from Benetton Sports and Tennis Centre, Allenton):

Expenditure

- Posters and flyers – £50
- Court hire – outdoor courts, including posts – £10 per court per evening × 6 evenings × 2 courts = £120
- Umpire costs – £20 per umpire per evening × 6 evenings × 2 umpires = £240
- Administration costs (e.g. timekeeper/administrator) – £10 × 6 = £60
- Medals (supplier = trophy direct) – only to second-place team – 10 × £5 = £50
- Trophies (supplier = trophy direct) – only to winning team – 10 × £10 = £100

Total – £620 over six-week period

Income

Each team to be charged weekly at £20 (£2 per person × 10 people in each team) × 6 teams × 6 weeks = £720.

The expenditure and income is balanced so the club covers its costs and doesn't make a loss. However, this balance depends on the number of teams joining the league. If fewer teams join, the club may need to source external funding.

Two courts are in poor condition: we need to consider costs of upgrading them if all teams can't be accommodated on the other two courts.

> You will need to consider all expenditure based on realistic costs. Ensure you know these figures before writing any proposal. You can research local projects or relevant websites to get an idea of realistic costs.

> If you struggle with maths you should revise these sorts of costs thoroughly before your exam.

> You will need to ensure that your expenditure does not exceed your income, ensuring that the final figure is balanced.

> Your resources should help you meet your aims and should be realistic.

Now try this

Write a list of resources you will need for your 'Back to Hockey' scheme to include in your proposal. Make sure that you include at least **two** for each type of resource: financial, physical and human.

Writing about wider sports development

You need to think about how your proposal could influence, or be influenced by the wider sports development context. You should consider issues such as sports development aims and organisations, infrastructure, environmental and economics issues and use of media.

When you justify something, you are supporting an opinion or proving something is right or reasonable. To do this, you need to use evidence.

'This Girl Can' is a Sport England initiative to increase women's participation in sport and physical activity.

Sample response extract

Current participation rates show that nationally 180 000 people aged 16+ are playing netball at least once a week (Active People Survey, Sport England 2016).

Promotional campaigns such as 'This Girl Can' and the 2012 Olympic legacy seem to have encouraged more people to get back into netball and attend sessions.

For my event to fit into these national initiatives, I wanted to make it easier for women to take up netball, socialise and play competitively. The six-week league would enable women to play 40 minutes of quality netball each week, coached and supported by Vulchers Netball Club and the local netball sports development officer. This would, I hope, enable those who would like to attend Vulchers 'Back to Netball' sessions to join in the winter leagues.

This proposal supports lifelong participation aims for creating a healthier nation (Sport England, Active Nation).

Include relevant research to support your aims.

Link the proposal to any relevant national initiatives and mission statements.

Make sure you refer to how your proposal fits in with the wider sports development context, such as improving mental and physical well-being.

Using the resources or website of the sport's national governing body is a useful way of sharing information about your project and its impact.

Always consider sustainability. How will this initiative continue without any external funding?

Sample response extract

In terms of media and commercialisation, I hope to continue to advertise and publish results, tournaments and any sessions the club runs on the club's webpages, on England Netball regional websites and in England Netball's quarterly magazine, which is distributed nationally. I also hope this event is the start of something more sustainable rather than being a standalone event.

Sample response extract

I hope my event will not only promote skills and knowledge, but also create a sustainable way for women to develop a healthier habit for life, bringing about lifelong participation in the game and helping people to make new friends as well as uniting communities.

This answer could also consider stakeholders such as politicians, and education and healthcare providers. What role will they play?

Sports development can have a positive impact on community cohesion.

At a local level, cultural considerations could include whether there are any cultural barriers to participation in hockey. Economic considerations could concern the use or development of facilities.

Now try this

1   One of the aims of England Hockey is to grow participation by making hockey more visible and accessible. How does your 'Back to Hockey' proposal support this aim?

2   Think about environmental, political, cultural and/or economic considerations – name one way your proposal will affect each of these areas, or be affected by them.

Types of sports and active leisure businesses

The sports and active leisure sector includes a wide range of businesses. Some are related to the community, while others are focused mostly on profit.

Private-sector businesses

These are owned by private individuals and groups and are mainly profit focused. Types include:

- **Sole traders** (e.g. personal trainers, sports massage therapists) – These businesses are owned and managed by one person who is legally responsible for their debt (this is called **unlimited liability**). Sole traders are common in the sports and active leisure industry.

- **Partnership** (e.g. design and sales of sportswear) – This type of business is formed when two or more people create a company and share all responsibilities (e.g. profit and debt). Partnerships can be **limited** or **unlimited** depending on how they have been registered.

- **Private limited company (Ltd)** (e.g. many gyms and sports equipment suppliers) – These are controlled by shareholders who invest in the company. The shares are controlled by a board of directors which appoints staff. Directors are only accountable for their investment; they are not responsible for any debts if the company fails.

- **Public limited company (plc)** (e.g. Manchester United) – These float shares on the open market (stock exchange), meaning anyone can buy them. Shareholders can vote on general policies and directors make a profit based on a dividend which is only paid if the company makes a profit.

- **Cooperative** (e.g. AFC Wimbledon) – This type of organisation is owned, managed and run for the benefit of its members. They can be any size, from a football club or social centre to a large sports retailer, and their liability depends on whether they are a society, limited company, partnership or plc.

Public-sector businesses

These are facilities and services that belong to the government and are managed by local or borough councils. They focus on providing a quality service within the available budget, not necessarily making a profit. They include:

- **Public corporation** – This may be either a publicly owned company or a state-owned organisation, such as a university (many universities extend their sports facilities for public use).

- **Local authority** – This is a business run by a local, district, city or borough council, which will have a sports and leisure brief to provide a range of services. Many gyms are run by local authorities, or by the local authority in partnership with a private company.

Third-sector businesses

These run for the benefit of society or the community, are not for profit and are not governmental. Types include:

- **Voluntary sector** – In a sports context, these are organisations that exist simply to provide opportunities to play and sometimes promote excellence. Most of those involved are not paid for their time and skills. They may be local sports-specific clubs (such as a town cricket club), and volunteers may be coaches, treasurers, scouts, kit washers and officials.

- **Charitable trusts** – These organisations exist to fulfil a common aim, such as improvement of public health via sports, and raise and/or donate money to further this aim. They do not usually pay tax.

SportsAid is an example of a **charitable trust**. It helps dedicated young athletes and performers to realise their full potential by supporting them financially with help towards training, transport, equipment and other items they need to succeed.

Now try this

Look at each of the following and identify what type of business they are (for example, limited company, charitable trust, cooperative):

- Sports Direct International (sporting goods retailer)
- Barcelona FC (football club)
- Freedom Leisure (gym and facilities management)
- Aspire Sports (children's sports activities)

Research why you think each business has chosen to be that type of company.

Scope and size of business activities

The scope of a business or organisation can be measured by the area to which it can offer its products and services. Its size is usually determined by the level of current or potential sales or demand, and can be measured by the number of staff involved.

Local – All activities are located within a few miles of the target market, customers or user/s.

Scope of business activities

National – Activities are available throughout the country. If a business operates only across the UK, it is also regarded as a national business.

Multinational – This relates to large companies that manufacture goods and/or offer services in several different countries all over the world, such as Adidas, Nike and Sports Direct.

International – Trade and activities are carried out in one or more countries. This has been made considerably easier since the advent of the internet.

Dunlop is a well-known British sports goods brand. It started as a local rubber goods manufacturer in 1889 and began to produce rubber golf balls at its Birmingham factory in 1910. It soon became known for its tennis and squash balls and rackets (shown here). It acquired the Slazenger brand in 1959. Since 1986, it has been owned by various international and multinational companies, including Sports Direct. Its head office is still in Derbyshire.

Sporting example

Park Resorts Leisure: franchising

Franchising is common in the sports and active leisure sector. For example, Park Resorts Leisure is a national business that employs thousands of people in several roles to offer leisure facilities all over the UK. Some branches might appear local but they are part of a franchise, where individuals or small businesses have paid Park Resorts Leisure to take responsibility for their local branch. There they sell products or services on Park Resort Leisure's behalf in return for a share of the profit. Other examples include Premier Sports or Tumble Tots.

Classifying businesses by size

Size	No. of staff	Example
Micro	Up to 9	Local gym run by owner/manager
Small	10–49	Leisure centre
Medium	50–249	Football League club
Large	250+	Sports retail chain

Although it doesn't always follow, micro and small businesses tend to be sole traders, partnerships and private limited companies, while large businesses may be private limited companies or plcs. Cooperatives can be any size.

Typical sizes of UK businesses

The UK parliament publishes reports on the contribution businesses make to the economy. It is hard to find specific data on businesses in sports and active leisure. The following data covers businesses in all fields:

- In 2014, there were 5.4 million private sector businesses in the UK.

- More than 99 per cent were not large businesses.

- Micro-, small or medium businesses employed around 15.6 million people (2015), this being about half of the UK workforce.

Now try this

Which types of business are most likely to be large?

Identify two businesses within each of the following fields of the sports and active leisure industry, and describe the scope of their activities.

- Sports and leisure, e.g. leisure centres, holiday parks, adventure and outdoor

- Sports science, e.g. sports psychologist

- Exercise and therapies, e.g. personal trainer

- Teaching and education, e.g. sports technician

Aims and objectives of the private sector

The aims and objectives of a business or organisation must be SMART: **Specific** (they say exactly what is meant), **Measurable** (it can be proved they have been met), **Achievable** (actions are possible), **Realistic** (they can be done) and **Time-constrained** (they have deadlines).

Aim/objective	Description	Sporting example
Making profit	The first and overarching principle of a commercial business is simply to make as much money as possible.	Chelsea Football Club profits from not only ticket sales, but global merchandising, player endorsements and broadcaster income.
Breaking even	To survive, a business must make enough money to cover its fixed costs (those that are constant no matter the level of business) and variable costs (those that change according to how well the business is doing).	A cricket coaching business that offers both its services and products (such as bats and clothing) has to bear certain fixed costs, such as rental on sports halls and pitches, and also variable costs, such as the number of bats sold. Its income must cover these costs to break even.
Surviving	A successful business will continue year after year. This may require reinventing or rebranding, even if it is outwardly successful, or it may risk being outdone by rivals.	Wakefield Trinity LFC is one of the oldest rugby league clubs but, in recent years, it has been threatened with winding-up orders and bankruptcy. To survive, it must rebrand, improve its stadium and relocate to satisfy Super League minimum rules.
Growth	A company does not have to expand to survive, but healthy, well-managed growth is a characteristic of a strong business. This can happen internally by using existing profits to grow, or externally by merging with or taking over another company.	Sports Direct International often grows by acquiring new brands, such as Karrimor, Carlton, No Fear and USA Pro.
Leading the market	A business that makes the most profit or has the greatest market share in a particular sector is the market leader.	Nike sells approximately 23 per cent of all sports shoes annually.
Diversification	This is when a business changes or adds to the products and services they already offer.	This includes football clubs have always made money from gate receipts, but since 2007 Manchester United has made more from global merchandising than ticket sales.
Providing services	This is the way in which a business offers certain services.	Football clubs that offer stadium tours, therapists who offer courses of treatment and coaches who offer one-to-one tuition.
Offering strong customer service and satisfaction	In a competitive industry, customers can quickly switch allegiance or compare the value offered by different businesses. Businesses go to great lengths to establish and maintain good relationships, particularly with repeat customers such as season ticket holders or regular clients.	Norwich City Football Club offers season ticket holders additional benefits such as discounts at restaurants, for Sky TV and at local businesses. It also keeps fans loyal with match-day extras such as meeting the players.

Now try this

Find a small, private-sector sports business that is local to you. Look at its website and/or talk to its owner and identify three SMART objectives that could help it to grow.

◀ Use the table to identify ways in which the business can develop.

Aims and objectives of the public and voluntary sectors

The aims of public and voluntary sectors are less focused on profit but still mindful of value for money. Rather than making a profit, these sectors focus on using funding efficiently and effectively to provide services that benefit people.

Aim/objective	Description	Sporting example
Controlling costs	As revenue (income) to the public sector is largely from tax, managers and politicians must exercise **cost control**, demonstrate accountability and spend the funds wisely.	If local authorities' budgets are cut, they have to decide how to spend their funds efficiently. They must show that they are running sports facilities, such as gyms, as efficiently as possible.
Value for money	Key considerations when ensuring **value for money** in public sports spending include: • providing services at the lowest cost • using resources to produce services • making the most efficient use of those resources.	Local authority leisure facilities such as swimming pools that are used by a school during the daytime, and by the public in the evening and at weekends, represent value for money to taxpayers as their use is being maximised.
Offering high-quality service	The services and facilities need to be as good as possible within the budget provided, as they are still being funded by taxpayers and other sources of public money.	Sport England has a National Benchmarking Service which routinely checks public sports and leisure provision. Key areas of these quality checks include cleanliness, accessibility and to what extent certain populations are provided for, such as the over 50s.
Meeting government standards	The *Code for Sports Governance* (2016) establishes a minimum set of standards of accountability for anyone who seeks public or lottery funding in sport. The core principles are a clear structure, the best people, transparent communication, high standards of integrity and conduct, and controlled policies and processes.	The code applies to all organisations in the UK to which UK Sport and Sport England provide grant funding, although the extent of compliance required depends on the size of the organisation.

Voluntary sector

Although organisations in the voluntary sector vary widely, their common aim is to benefit communities or individuals within those communities. A local tennis club might encourage members to improve their health and well-being. A children's swimming club's main aim might be to teach children to swim and to ensure they know how to be safe in the water.

 parkrun

parkrun is a not-for-profit company funded by grants and commercial sponsors with the aim of making running easy, fun and sociable. It depends on thousands of local volunteers to organise free, weekly 5 km runs in locations around the UK and beyond.

Now try this

You should also consider the ethics behind your objectives.

Identify SMART objectives for each of the following:
• UK Sport
• parkrun
• a local sports club

How do they compare with the ones you drew up for private-sector companies?

Provision of services and their purpose

Services that are offered in the UK are many and varied. It is important to understand both the kinds of programmes on offer and the reasons why these kinds of service are offered.

Individual training – A person is offered advice or guidance and allowed to self-regulate, and to determine their own type of exercise and its pace and intensity (e.g. a gym programme, regular walking, or gardening).

Group exercise activities – These can include high-intensity dance or exercise, e.g. Zumba or spin cycling, or more sedate activities like yoga or Pilates.

Educational and school programmes
Schools offer **physical education** (PE) and sports clubs during, and out of, school hours. As well as traditional sports (e.g. football, athletics), schools with the facilities may run yoga, boxfit, Zumba, dance, cheerleading and martial arts classes.

Water-based activities – These vary according to the audience, but most public pools offer aqua aerobics or swim fit. Open-air and sea swimming are also on the increase.

Health and fitness programmes
These are aimed at everyone but often targeted at those who need them the most, in a gym, outdoors, at a swimming pool or at home.

Gym programmes
Depending on users' needs and demands, gyms can be used independently by individuals, or for structured for weight/resistance classes (e.g. Zumba, step, treadmill, circuits, kettle bells and suspension classes; Tai Chi; core/workouts, abdominal workouts).

Programmes to promote participation

Programmes to enable demand
Some classes tap into current trends to encourage participation, e.g. high-intensity interval training workouts (HIIT), barre classes or Clubbercise.

Programmes to serve specific groups
These are usually cardiovascular or lower-intensity exercise programmes for targeted users (e.g. older adults; disabled people; antenatal and postnatal women; children and young people; referred patients with obesity, cardiac, pulmonary or metabolic disease, or other long-term conditions).

Swimming pool programmes
As well as traditional swimming and exercise classes, swimming pools can also make use of the weight-bearing nature of water to offer rehabilitation programmes. These involve simple mobility and flexibility exercises that assist those returning from injury or with limited mobility.

Sports programmes

This type of participation programme differs from sport to sport but generally includes:

- ✓ coaching sessions from beginners to elite
- ✓ taster sessions
- ✓ teaching coaching
- ✓ teaching officiation/refereeing
- ✓ skills-improvement clinics and residential camps
- ✓ social sports programmes for groups, such as 50-plus mornings
- ✓ survival and extreme sports, and challenging endurance events such as Tough Mudder
- ✓ outdoor and adventurous activities.

Services and facilities

The sports sector is competitive and customers have many choices. To attract and keep them, organisations and sports facilities may offer services other than exercise instruction, such as therapeutic or sports massages, or extra facilities such as a café, free car parking, clean and spacious changing areas, meeting rooms, spa facilities, secure lockers or a crèche.

Many gyms are focused on providing excellent customer service, ensuring that members feel welcome and relaxed. This is often measured via online surveys of members' experiences of staff and facilities.

Consider how to provide a balanced programme that is accessible and practical as well as varied and interesting.

Now try this

Research and identify suitable classes, facilities and services for a small sports area in the basement of an office block. Consider the needs of the office staff, for example the times they can attend, suitable one-to-one programmes, types of activities and how to encourage regular members.

Customer groups: demographics and purpose

Our society is complex and businesses must consider factors such as demographics (statistical data relating to the population and characteristics of different groups), changes in household structure, religion and culture, education, ethics, and attitudes to work and family life. Drawing on these factors, they will identify specific groups as potential users.

Demographics

As the population in the UK increases, so too do different groups in that society. Here are some examples of how this affects sports provision:

- **Age** – A growing area of the sporting economy is the provision of activities for the over 50s ('the Grey Pound').

- **Gender** – Businesses recognise the opportunities of more women taking part in regular exercise (for example via energy drinks, women's-only events and gyms, high-end sports fashion).

- **Ethnicity** – To be competitive, sports businesses must recognise and accept cultural and religious differences.

- **Disability** – Businesses increasingly acknowledge, understand and tackle the barriers that many disabled people face, by offering specialised equipment and improving access. The UK's success in many Paralympic sports reflects this.

- **Socio-economic** – The importance of enabling social mobility is reflected in Corporate Social Responsibility (CSR) programmes. Manchester United Football Club works with schools and local communities to reduce racism and improve respect for others.

Purpose

It is critical that sports businesses recognise why their customers want to participate.

- **Recreation** – Many people carry out physical activity, sport or exercise for fun. Part of the appeal of parkrun is the social aspect, as it is for walkers and cyclists.

- **Weight loss** – Weight control is key for many people taking part in physical activity, whether this is through simple exercise routines like walking, dancing or gardening, or organised classes and memberships.

- **Personal image** – Some people do physical activity simply to look good. Sport has been used to promote fashion and cosmetics for years.

- **Health maintenance** – Regular sports participation helps to maintain health and well-being in the longer term, which is a useful factor for gym managers and exercise providers who want to retain members and customers.

- **Training for performance** – Staying competitive is vital for thousands of professional, semi-professional or amateur sports people.

- **Charity** – Businesses' reputations benefit from sponsoring and supporting large or local charity events.

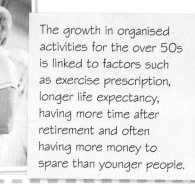

The growth in organised activities for the over 50s is linked to factors such as exercise prescription, longer life expectancy, having more time after retirement and often having more money to spare than younger people.

Since the 1980s, the London Marathon has enabled thousands of runners to raise millions of pounds for charity.

Research current advice about safe and effective training for Muslims during Ramadan.

Now try this

As British Muslims, Moeen Ali, Mo Farah and Amir Khan observe Ramadan, when they cannot eat or drink from dawn until dusk. This presents issues for them related to training and competing. If you were a business advisor, what products and services would you offer to make this less of a challenge for these and other Muslim sportspeople?

Meeting customer needs

The quality of staff and their attitude and skills can be the difference between a successful and an unsuccessful business. Staff are also key in determining whether the provision of goods or services is acceptable or could be improved.

Staffing

Human resources factors to consider include ensuring that:

- there are sufficient staff to deliver the products/services
- the staff are suitably qualified and competent to perform their roles
- the staff are mindful of health and safety
- the staff are working to the best of their ability
- the staff adopt and reflect the company aims and objectives.

For example:

- Personal trainers need to be able to adapt workouts to participants' wishes or physical needs. They may use their knowledge of nutrition or anatomy to customise training.
- A swimming pool that does not invest in training lifeguards will soon discover that the core business cannot operate without them.
- Reception and office staff should put customer service at the core of their role, but first-aid knowledge might also be an advantage.

Provision

There are several ways in which customers can become dissatisfied with the products or services on offer. Not all of them will complain; some simply switch to another business. Generally, customers should expect:

- **good service** based on reputation – such as replace or exchange policies for sports goods

Customer feedback might be via testimonies, word of mouth or on social media. Often this affects reputation positively or negatively.

- **reliable service** – a consistently good record of providing what is promised
- **options** – for example, offering a range of other classes when one exercise class is cancelled, or an alternative when a tennis racket is out of stock
- **responsiveness** – the business acknowledges and acts on enquiries and feedback, good or bad
- **continual improvement** – for example, upgrading gym equipment, offering new products and services, maintaining facilities.

Legal requirements

All businesses are bound by certain laws that protect consumers. In particular, they must be aware of:

- The Consumer Rights Act 2015 – This covers product quality, returning goods, repairs and replacements, digital content rights, delivery rights and supplying a service.
- The Consumer Credit Act 1974 – This regulates spending, and gives consumers a cooling-off period if they change their mind.
- The Health and Safety at Work etc Act 1974 – This covers general duties to ensure the safety of users of facilities.

A fitness facility or gym with an aggressive membership sales policy could not only lose its reputation but also find itself on the wrong side of the law.

Now try this

As a newly appointed sales assistant at your local gym, you have been asked to present your ideas about how to sell membership without being too aggressive. Outline your approach, how to present the membership options, how to sign someone up on the day and how to include a built-in cooling-off period.

You would need to balance meeting recruitment targets with not pushing potential members too hard.

Stakeholders

Every sports business has stakeholders (anyone who affects or influences a business). This could be a direct influence, such as a manager within the business, or an indirect influence, such as a supplier who provides branded uniform for staff in a sports coaching business.

Examples of internal stakeholders

Managers – responsible for the actions of other employees; they recruit staff, plan future directions and manage day-to-day activities

Employees – report to the managers and carry out specific roles e.g. lifeguards, leisure attendants, cleaners, sports coaches, maintenance staff

> **Those generally employed within the organisation**
> for example at a fitness centre

Owners/shareholders – have overall responsibility for the business and some recruitment; usually also provide funding for wages and facilities

Fitness centres need employees with very different skills who will work as a team if the business is to be successful.

Examples of external stakeholders

Suppliers – those who supply materials or services to the business, e.g. massage oil, towels, specialist treatment equipment

Competitors – other sports therapists and other therapist types such as osteopaths, particularly nearby

Customers – paying clients

Creditors – those who lend money or offer materials in advance of payment, e.g. agencies, room rental, laundry services

> **Those not employed by a business but critical to its success**
> for example, a sports therapist sole trader

Government – makes laws that need to be followed, controls taxes, offers start-up funding, and so on

Fundraisers – often individuals or small groups who raise funds for participation, facilities or services; regulated sources of public and private funding can be found at a County Sports Partnership

Interest groups – may be specific to the business (e.g. a sports therapy continuing professional development (CPD) group) or more general (e.g. a Facebook group of people who have benefited from sports therapy)

Trade associations and professional bodies – represent members and uphold standards (e.g. The Society of Sports Therapists, The Sports Therapy Association)

Communities – may be immediate neighbours concerned about parking, or demand in the wider community for sports therapy

Sports therapists must develop relationships with various external stakeholders including banks, accountants, laundries, hotels, landlords and customers.

Trade associations

These are a group of businesses within a specific sector, working together to improve standards for members. They can be important and vocal external stakeholders. Sport is not as rich in these as other sectors but the Federation of Sports and Play Associations (FSPA) is a trade body that represents manufacturers of sports and play equipment, helping to ensure minimum standards in trading and safety. Other examples include the Sports and Physical Education Association UK (SPE) and the British Golf Industry Association (BGIA).

Now try this

As an experienced paintballer, you would like to set up an adventure sports business that includes not only paintball but also archery tag, laser tag, swordplay and other activities. Review the potential internal and external stakeholders.

To help identify stakeholders, consider venues, facilities, customer base and hours of operation.

Laws, legislation and safeguarding

Sports businesses, like all others, should operate within the law. If they do not, this can result in fines or even convictions and imprisonment for company directors. There are several considerations with regards to the law, including equality and diversity, safeguarding, data protection, health and safety, and employment.

Equality and diversity

The **Equality Act 2010** makes it an offence to discriminate against anyone based on their:

- age
- disability
- gender reassignment
- marriage or civil partnership status
- race
- religion or beliefs
- sex
- sexual orientation.

Safeguarding

This concerns protecting children and/or vulnerable adults, for example from abuse by a sports teacher or coach.

The Children Act 1989 helps to protect such customers in sports businesses. Companies are required by law to check whether staff are suitable to work with children and vulnerable adults using the Disclosure Barring Service (DBS).

The Department for Education has published statutory guidance on supervising children's activities to meet the **Safeguarding Vulnerable Groups Act 2006**.

Health and safety

Employers must take responsibility for the health and safety of their employees. The **Health and Safety at Work etc Act 1974** requires staff to receive training in:

- safe practice
- handling of chemicals (where necessary)
- lifting and manual handling (where necessary)
- evacuation procedures.

Visitors and customers are also protected under this law.

Health and safety must be observed at all times when dealing with customers and staff.

Employment

When recruiting staff, an employer must be aware of the following legal issues:

- Equality in recruitment
- Requirement to publish gender pay gaps
- National living wage
- National Insurance
- Statutory maternity, paternity and sickness pay rates
- Protection for apprentices
- Illegal working/right to work

Data protection

This is about an individual's right to privacy, online or otherwise.

The Data Protection Act 1998 protects personal data such as medical details, addresses, bank details and references. Employers who disclose this information carelessly or maliciously can be prosecuted.

Now try this

Devise a code of safe practice for a trampoline park.

Research relevant health and safety law. ROSPA is a good place to start (www.rospa.com).

Business models: SWOT analysis

An established way of looking at the relationship between a business and its marketing environment is a SWOT analysis.

Strengths, Weaknesses, Opportunities and Threats

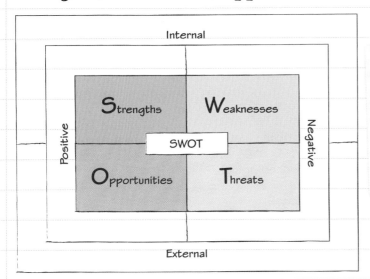

SWOT analysis looks at the business's current and future position. This can sometimes be done quickly, with information that is already known, but more details may require further research. Being aware of strengths, weaknesses, opportunities and threats can help a business to focus its strategy.

Strengths

These are areas that are an advantage because they are different from those of other businesses.

Strengths of a personal trainer might include:

- transferable people skills that make it easier to win new clients and deal with stakeholders
- the endorsement of celebrity clients
- being in an area where the population has high disposable income.

Weaknesses

These are internal aspects that are not going as well or could be improved to support the success of the business.

Weaknesses of a personal trainer might include:

- a lack of experience in marketing
- a damaged reputation after a client was injured while using a machine
- a poor website and weak communications with potential clients.

Opportunities

These are markets that enable the business to be successful.

Opportunities for a personal trainer might include:

- a hotel with a private exercise room for hire to treat both current clients and hotel guests
- forming a partnership with colleagues in sports therapy and related fields to offer more services at more venues
- a situation where a competitor has moved away, leaving clients looking for a new trainer.

Threats

These may be external competitors or pricing that could damage overall performance.

Threats for a personal trainer might include:

- a new competitor opening a business two miles away
- a price war with a competitor (great for the customers but not for business!)
- new taxes or taxation rules.

You could make up specific details but also research similar real businesses and note their range of classes, services and products.

Now try this

You are an experienced and qualified swimming instructor who has moved to a new town and notice that hardly any swimming teaching or coaching is available at its two swimming pools. Devise a SWOT analysis to identify if this is a viable business idea.

Business models: PESTLE analysis (1)

A PESTLE analysis is a strategic tool that helps a business establish how external factors are likely to influence its success and operations.

How it works

A PESTLE analysis involves considering **six external factors**, and assessing how they might impact the operations of the business. Once a business has analysed these six factors it can use this information to:

- conduct market research
- identify and exploit new opportunities
- identify and protect against threats.

Six factors

 P – Political

 E – Economic

 S – Social

 T – Technological

 L – Legal

 E – Environmental

You can revise factors 3 to 6 from this list on the next page.

1 Political factors

It is important for businesses to understand trends in international, national and local government. An example of a political factor that could affect a sporting business includes access to government spending or local authority grants.

Sporting example Sport England allocates grants which are determined by perceived political need. 'This Girl Can', funded by Sport England, aims to encourage female participation in sport by providing better awareness, facilities and role models.

Brexit is an example of a **political factor**. After leaving the EU it might be harder for the UK to export merchandise because of poor exchange rates, or for a sports team to play exhibition games in Europe, because there may be less freedom of movement.

2 Economic factors

When the economy is strong, people are more likely to spend money and banks are more likely to lend it. In times of recession, people are more cautious in spending their disposable income. Other economic factors could include:

- tax rates
- interest rates
- inflation
- employment figures
- currency exchange rates.

Three examples of economic factors in sport

1. When interest rates are low, it would be a good time for a personal trainer to borrow money and invest in equipment and resources.

2. An increase in the duty (tax) on fuel will have a direct negative impact on businesses that consume a lot of energy, such as swimming pools.

3. When public money is limited, local authorities are most likely to cut 'less important' services like sport and leisure.

Now try this

Give reasons that relate specifically to the business of a fitness centre.

While conducting a PESTLE analysis, a fitness centre discovers that its local authority is launching a scheme to encourage adult participation in team sports. Explain how this could:

1. pose a threat to the fitness centre's existing business   2. provide a new business opportunity.

Business models: PESTLE analysis (2)

The remaining elements of a PESTLE analysis are **Social**, **Technological**, **Legal** and **Environmental**.

③ Social factors

Sports businesses must understand the diverse needs of their customers.

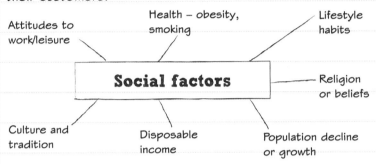

- Attitudes to work/leisure
- Health – obesity, smoking
- Lifestyle habits
- Religion or beliefs
- Culture and tradition
- Disposable income
- Population decline or growth

Social factors

④ Technological factors

Business is influenced by technology, by research and innovation, by the age and suitability of available technology, and by emerging technology such as virtual reality. Other factors to consider are:

- improved global communication
- virtual meetings
- 24-hour sales online
- pressure to respond quickly
- online crime, such as fraudulent use of customer data
- increased global competition.

Sporting example Opening a Rugby Union coaching academy in north-west England may overlook the history and culture of Rugby League in that region, and the business could suffer.

Virtual reality (VR) is an example of a **technological factor**. It is often used in professional training for sports including football, baseball, American football, golf and athletics.

⑤ Legal factors

Companies must trade within the law, so a working knowledge of all relevant laws, both in the UK and potentially internationally, is vital. The key considerations are:

- employment law
- tax law
- legal business structure
- laws concerning how businesses can operate.

⑥ Environmental factors

Not only do sporting businesses need to think about their impact on the environment, they also need to consider what impact the environment could have on their business.

- Climate, weather and seasons
- Transport links
- Generation of waste and recycling

Environmental factors

 Sporting example A sailing school will only be able to operate safely in calm weather, which means that it must consider the likelihood of storms and high winds.

Now try this

Conduct a PESTLE analysis on a sports club near you.

Job roles and person specifications

This page describes some of the main roles in the sports and active leisure industry and explores how job descriptions and person specifications help employers to find the right staff.

Executive/owner/manager(s) – has overall responsibility for the business or, if a manager, responsibility for a part of the business or team

Supervisor(s) – deals with day-to-day issues that arise on site, from customers or from the team

Qualified sports leader – plans and runs sports activities; often the customer-facing part of the business

Instructor – usually leads activities in outdoor environments such as climbing, canoeing, mountain biking

Typical roles in the sports and active leisure industry

Support staff – may include security, cleaners and office-based staff such as IT support and administrators

Volunteer – a person who gives up their spare time to help, because of their enthusiasm, or to meet the requirements of a qualification like The Duke of Edinburgh Award Scheme

Trainee – someone new to a role, who is still learning how to do it so is supervised more closely

Coach – a qualified, competent sports specialist leader, for example, basketball, cricket, trampoline gymnastics, rugby.

Sporting example In an outdoor and adventure centre, the staff structure could be:

- **Manager** – has overall responsibility for the effective running of the centre, staffing issues, programmes and customer liaison
- **Supervisors** – oversee instructors and have responsibility for e.g. stock inventories, ordering, shift rotas
- **Instructors** – plan, deliver and evaluate outdoor sessions such as climbing; are responsible for safety, learning and enjoyment
- **Administrators (office staff)** – take residential bookings and liaise with schools, colleges or other customers
- **Security** – make sure that the residents are safe
- **Cleaners** – keep the shower areas, drying rooms, accommodation and eating areas up to standard
- **IT staff** – manage IT infrastructure and maintain website.

Person specifications and job descriptions

Person specifications provide information on the ideal person for the job and might include:

- attainments or qualifications
- previous experience
- personal skills, for example willing to work in a team or undertake training
- special skills or aptitudes.

Job descriptions focus on providing specifics about the job such as:

- job title
- manager's role
- scope of the role
- typical tasks and activities
- salary
- responsibilities
- department and location.

These documents provide a context for the role, indicating its level of decision-making, responsibility and accountability. They will form the basis of the recruitment and selection process so that all applicants can be assessed against the same criteria.

Now try this

Research a sports job that interests you, such as lifeguard, canoeing instructor or fitness instructor.

1 Identify:
   (a) the skills and experience you already have that meet the role
   (b) the skills and experience you do not yet have or you need to develop.
2 Make a brief action plan describing how you would approach filling these skills gaps so that you are more suitable for the job.

 Links Make your action plan SMART (see page 44).

Many employment websites like leisureopportunities.co.uk or UK Sport have sports-specific job descriptions.

Types of employment

The sports and active leisure sector offers varied opportunities and types of employment.

Types of working patterns

	Description	Benefits	Risks
Full-time e.g. leisure centre manager	Work organised over 35+ hours per week	Maximises income	• Restricts non-work time available for family, leisure and household tasks
Part-time e.g. cricket umpire, school PE provider	Work organised over fewer than 35 hours per week	Flexible hours, e.g. around school hours	• May not earn sufficient income • May not be possible to fulfil role in time available
Seasonal e.g. ski instructor	Work available only at certain times of year owing to weather conditions	Flexible and interesting opportunities for those without commitments	• Not a continuous source of income so could be difficult for those with families and financial commitments

Types of role

	Description	Benefits	Risks
Consultant	External expert advisor who charges for a service like delivering training or producing support material	• Enables staff to be trained in specialist knowledge, such as first aid, customer service, sports-specific techniques • Consultant can focus on sharing and developing their specific skill area	• Can be expensive, limiting employment opportunities • Consultant needs to keep up with current trends and knowledge
Volunteer	Someone who gives up their time for free to carry out a role	• Can lead to paid employment and is often a first step in the sports industry • Opportunity to learn new skills, feel good about yourself and offer a valuable service	• Many sports/events depend on unpaid stewards, coaches, kit washers, fixtures secretaries and officials • Some roles are less popular, e.g. treasurers
Franchisee e.g. trampoline parks	Someone who has bought the right to sell an established sport or play facility with brand's products or services, in return for a share of the profits.	• A proven market • Brand reputation, support and processes already in place	• Investment may not pay off • Still requires work to establish business in target market

Examples of seasonal jobs include ski and snowboard instructors, outdoor activity instructors, football referees, open-water lifeguards, and coaches, leaders and instructors at holiday parks.

Among the many sports and leisure franchising opportunities are baby swimming clubs, go-karting, kick-boxing, gyms, play centres, trampoline parks, indoor ski centres and children's sports coaching.

Now try this

Research sport volunteering opportunities in your area. Make a shortlist of the top three that appeal to you and justify your choices.

Sport England has an established commitment to supporting volunteers in sport. Look at its website for ideas.

Human resource management

People are one of the most important resources in a business but, like any resource, they need to be managed. Salaries, timetabling and conditions of employment are particularly important.

What is human resource management?

Human resource (HR) management tasks range from recruiting and appraising staff to implementing policies and ensuring conditions of employment are followed.

Large businesses may have an HR team but in smaller businesses this role may be undertaken by the owner, manager or even coaches.

HR management must balance the needs of the business with the preferences of the staff and the requirements of the law in order to meet the business's overall aims and objectives.

Salaries

Deciding and paying salaries is an HR task. The person setting salaries must consider:

- the budget available
- the seniority of the role and its responsibilities
- how it compares with competitors
- the amount of money people doing that role would expect to receive
- legal restrictions such as the minimum or living wage for different age groups
- whether there can be any leeway if the person chosen for the role negotiates the figure.

Timetabling staff

Staff must be available when customers need them, so one HR job is to ensure the right staff are there at the right time. In a gym, this might mean a shift pattern where receptionists and trainers work during busy periods, such as early mornings, evenings or weekends. A first aider might also need to be on the premises. As well as taking staff availability into account, timetabling is also influenced by laws that determine the maximum hours that can be worked within a set period.

Few jobs in the sports and leisure industry are 9–5. For example, many sports coaches are needed in the early morning.

Conditions of employment

Employees should receive a written statement of the conditions of their employment. This states the:

- name of employer and employee
- date employment started
- job description/job title
- job location
- rate of pay and when the employee will be paid
- working hours
- holiday entitlement
- other important details relating to the role.

What is expected of the employee?

In return for pay and benefits, the employee will be expected to:

- work an agreed number of hours and turn up on time
- fulfil the role specified in the job description
- undertake training as necessary
- behave appropriately.

If they do not, HR policies may mean that they are disciplined or, if they continue not to fulfil their role, dismissed (sacked). Laws are in place to help reduce unfair dismissals.

Pay scales change all the time, but factors such as experience and level of responsibility affect how much an individual is paid.

Now try this

Research the common salaries for different jobs in the sports and active leisure industry. Explain why some jobs command more money than others.

Physical resources: planning and maintenance

Physical resources needed depend on the nature and size of the sports business – a sports centre requires large premises whereas a personal trainer may not need any! Either way, resources must be planned and maintained appropriately to keep the business running.

Resource planning

- **Supplies and materials** could include massage oils, business cards and stationery, tables and chairs, tackle bags and sports coaching equipment, vehicles, IT hardware and software, and specialist equipment.
- **Tasks** that the business is unable to do itself can be **contracted out** to others.

> • A swimming coach might need someone to collect money and do some administration.
>
> - A fitness centre might keep a list of reliable instructors to call if needed quickly.

- **Changes in staffing needs** can be foreseen when planning ahead, for example needing more staff in the summer, or identifying a specialist role. Existing staff may need extra training to use new equipment or products, such as kayaks, kettle bells or hydraulic couch.
- **Events and foreseen risk control** – Risk management in sports businesses is especially important because customers are physically moving or taking part in high-risk activities. Some risks are obvious, such as the need for first aid or safeguarding children, so should be planned for. Risk assessment should be suitable and sufficient for the activities.

> • Leaders of an overnight hike must complete a risk assessment and constantly re-evaluate that assessment during the hike.
>
> - A children's play facility needs to balance the likelihood of accidents against encouraging participants to actively enjoy and explore the area.

Resource maintenance

- **Emergency cover** refers to a backup in the case of a failure to supply goods or services.

> A tennis coach has a backup court in case the one they normally use is waterlogged.

- **Health and safety** – It is a legal and moral obligation to ensure equipment is safe and premises have adequate ventilation, fire exits, muster points and serviced firefighting equipment.

> Hygiene must be observed by a sports therapist to avoid cross infection.

- **Assets** are the items required to run a business, such as a vehicle, specialist equipment, massage couch, or computer. Instead of buying equipment, fitness companies often use **leasing options** to hire machines and equipment which are serviced and maintained by the hire company for a regular fee.
- **Maintenance and refurbishment** – Buying equipment can involve a large initial outlay and it needs to be maintained according to the manufacturer's guidelines. Refurbishment restores old or broken items. Both can be expensive.
- **Budgetary restraints** may limit the ability to buy, hire or maintain the resources a business wants or needs, so it has to decide how best to manage its finances.

> A squash coach might set a monthly or annual budget that includes all potential outlays such as rackets, balls, court fees and other expenses. Spending within the budget makes achieving profit targets easier.

Now try this

Research the costs of fitting out a gym within the following parameters:

- A £40 000 budget to cover all equipment including flooring and mirrors.
- A limit of 20 pieces of gym equipment and some free weights.
- Maintenance of equipment including tools.

Note as many variables as you can, for example the comparative costs of leasing or buying equipment over three years.

Importance of resource management

Resources can be human, physical or financial. The way in which sports businesses manage these complex variables will determine their success.

Maximising skills

Members of staff are a business's most important asset. Sometimes it is necessary to make the most of available resources.

- **Upskill** – A canoeing instructor could be easily trained to be redeployed as a kayak instructor or sailing instructor, at less cost than recruiting a new instructor.
- **Train in-house** – Instead of paying for a series of individual training sessions in a new sports therapy technique, it might be more cost effective for the team to be trained together in a single session on site.

Productivity

Sometimes a business must consider how productive and efficient it is. There are many ways to improve productivity.

A netball coach might:

- set aside time for administrative tasks such as invoicing, replying to emails, and other communications
- use a to-do list and cross tasks off regularly
- focus on what is important daily and avoid trying to do too much at once
- keep on top of social media without being distracted by it.

Capacity

This is a business's ability to respond to demand in terms of, for example, staff, time or ability of IT team to support the website.

If a fitness instructor is paid by the number of clients they have, they may take on too much work, rush and cut corners, resulting in injuries or lost clients. They should realistically estimate their capacity to offer the best service.

Reducing risk

There are ways a sports business might reduce the risk of poor performance, to help clarify the direction of the business.

A school sports coaching business might:

- have a plan for each part of the business
- consult other professionals, e.g. on a sports coaching business forum
- identify any issues linked to expanding coverage to more schools
- have a contingency plan for when things go wrong.

Reducing costs

Some costs are inevitable but must be limited where practically possible. Accounts should be checked regularly and areas of overspend identified and reduced.

A Pilates instructor working in their own facility would identify start-up costs such as equipment, rent for premises, marketing costs and utility bills.

Reducing waste

Not only does reducing waste maximise profit, but it is also an ethically sound approach. There are tough laws on those who don't manage waste properly.

A swimming pool facility could:

- reduce packaging and recycle all waste
- measure the amount of energy use (high in swimming pools)
- cover the pool when not in use to reduce energy consumption by up to a third
- eliminate bottled water.

Now try this

JSC Sports Coaching wants to run children's day-courses in the school holidays. They have two members of staff and do not have their own premises. Identify what resources they need and how they can run the courses successfully.

Marketing: 7 Ps (1)

The marketing mix is a framework for developing marketing plans. One widely accepted tool is the 7 Ps – how product, price, promotional mix, place, people, process and physical environment can be used to encourage customers to buy products and services. This page looks at the first three in the context of a sports business.

Product

This is what is sold – goods or services, experiences or events. Businesses must consider:

- **product life cycles** – how long will people want to buy it?
- **unique selling point (USP)** – what makes it special and unrivalled?
- **product range** – what other products fit together to cover all the market opportunities?

Sporting example: The Wimbledon tour

This is a successful business linked to an international tournament by offering tours of the Wimbledon tennis grounds. Its product life cycle is likely to last as long as the tournament is popular. Its USP is that there is only one Wimbledon! It increases its product range with a large gift shop and membership options.

Price

This is the amount of money that people pay for the product. It can take some skill to get it right. Pricing strategies include:

- **loss leaders** – selling a product/service at low cost to encourage people to spend more on other items
- **penetration pricing** – selling a product cheaply at first but raising the price once a customer base is established
- **skimming** – when the price for a product is set high but then reduced so that customers perceive value.

When BT Sport wants to encourage more subscribers for sports packages, it sometimes practises penetration pricing by offering a low-cost or even free subscription for a time before increasing the cost when customers have started to enjoy the service.

Promotional mix

This is any activity designed to raise awareness of a business, such as advertising, sales promotion and public relations. Key terms include:

- **digital promotion** – using electronic media such as smart phones, tablets or electronic billboards
- **social media** – conducting campaigns on sites like Snapchat, Instagram and Twitter
- **target market** – using certain media to target specific demographic groups
- **brand image** – using customers' positive associations with the company or product name
- **above the line** – promotion that uses mass media, e.g. newspapers, TV advertisements
- **below the line** – more targeted promotion, e.g. search engine marketing, leafleting, telemarketing.

Celebrity endorsement is using high profile celebrities such as sportsmen and women to sell products. In 2016, golfer Rory McIlroy earned more than £27 million in endorsements, before even picking up a golf club. Brands included Nike, Bose, EA Sports, Omega and Upper Deck.

Now try this

Identify a variety of sports businesses with successful marketing campaigns. Referring to the 7 Ps, what methods have they used and how have they targeted their market?

Research sports businesses of different sizes and compare their approaches.

Marketing: 7 Ps (2)

This page explores the remaining parts of the marketing mix – place, people, process and physical environment – sometimes known as the extended marketing mix.

Place

This is how products find their way to the consumer. Consider these examples:

- **Supply chains** are the process of getting a product from the manufacturer to the customer. For example, a tennis ball must first be manufactured and delivered to a wholesaler, who in turn sells to retailers, who then complete the chain with the consumer – the tennis player.

- **Logistics** describes the flow of physical goods to the consumer – the practicalities and arrangements needed to support the supply chain.

- **Customer trends** regarding place could include whether they prefer to receive their sports massage at home, or how likely they are to buy a product online instead of at a shop.

People

People are vital to service delivery. A single example of poor customer service can have a serious impact on a sports business.

- **Staff training** – This can affect the way in which a company operates. Competent, consistent staff are more likely to retain customers.

- **Consistent and reliable customer service** – Knowing what kind of service to expect can improve customer experience and will help to determine whether they keep coming back. Sports coaches can be technically excellent but if they can't relate to people then this will be bad for business.

- **Relationship between people and brand image** – If a brand's key values are friendliness and skills, these must be consistently reflected by the staff.

Process

When customers use a service, they take part in a series of processes. A new gym user will need an induction to learn how to use the equipment safely and effectively.

- **Managing customer interactions consistently** – Does everyone receive the same service? Do they have to wait? Can they all try the equipment?

- **Mode of service consumption** – How is the induction delivered? What is the physical experience? What is the perception of value – is the gym induction worth the money and time?

Gym inductions are often a customer's first experience of using the facility, so it is critical that staff provide a consistent process to encourage members to return.

Physical environment

This is about the place itself – the gym, football pitch or climbing wall, and areas like receptions, toilets and changing rooms.

- **Reflecting brand image in the physical environment** – Is it easily recognisable as belonging to the brand? Is it up to standard?

- **Appropriateness to offering** – is it a comfortable area, with enough space?

Sporting example

Balancing customer needs

The cost of high-quality gym changing rooms has to be reflected in the cost of membership. The business must consider whether customers are prepared to pay more for a luxurious environment or whether they would be happy to use a standard changing room for less cost. Factors such as cleanliness need to be ensured either way.

Now try this

Include your reasons for selecting the products or services over those of the competitors.

Think about your last major and minor sports purchases, for example equipment, an exercise class, or a membership subscription. Which of the 7 Ps encouraged you to choose that product, service or business?

Customer services and meeting customer needs

The benefits of customer service are obvious – if you are good at it you gain and keep customers, and if you are not, you do not. This page describes how a particular sporting business – a gymnastics centre – covers two key components of effective customer care.

Being knowledgeable about the offering

You would expect gym coaches to be both technically competent and qualified, but staff should also know about the wider context of customer experience.

- **Activities and services** – Staff should know about the gym's full range of services (e.g. teaching and coaching, competition training, performance analysis, after-school clubs, parkour sessions, sports massage or adult taster sessions) and recommend the most suitable service for each customer.

- **Equipment** – Staff should be trained in how to use and move equipment safely, whether this is basic mats or technical items like uneven bars or IT equipment for video analysis.

- **Facilities** – The premises covers not just the activity area but also reception and changing facilities. These should reflect the ethos of the business (e.g. clean, accessible) and staff should ensure they can answer customers' questions about them.

Highlighting the benefits of promotions

While promotional activities help a business to make money, they can also be an advantage to customers, for example by helping them save money. Consider the following examples:

- **Special offers** – These attract new businesses or reward loyalty. They could include a discount for early bookings or a free leotard with a 10-week course booking.

- **Customer loyalty schemes** – In the same way that a supermarket offers loyalty schemes, a sports business can reward returning customers. For example, it may offer a free class after every eight that are paid for, or discounted membership for customers that represent the club in a competition. This keeps customers coming back in a competitive market.

- **Open days** – Many gyms offer free taster sessions, where customers can try out the courses and facilities for free. Sometimes these are combined with raffles or giveaways.

Reception areas should be both inviting and functional.

Gymnastics businesses often provide courses for children, but promotions must also appeal to their parents, who will be paying!

Now try this

Using the examples provided, devise a customer care policy for the gymnastics centre. Include required staff knowledge levels about the services, equipment, activities and facilities and suitable promotions that would benefit the types of customer likely to attend.

You could consider it from the point of view of a particular staff member, such as a coach or personal trainer.

Communicating with customers

Anyone representing a sports business must adapt their communication by understanding customers' needs (empathy). Different situations often require different types of communication and skills.

Taking the initiative

Customers may not know what the business can offer, or have a problem they cannot solve by themselves, so staff will need to take the lead in the communication. They should consider:

- identifying what the customer needs to know, or the best way to solve their problem
- who is the best person to provide the information
- the most effective way of providing the information
- ways of promoting additional products or services (e.g. 'Were you aware that we now offer …?')
- the limits of their role (e.g. knowing the point at which to involve a manager).

Verbal communication

Speaking is the most direct method of verbal communication, for example when instructing a class, making safety announcements, using a telephone for taking bookings or welcoming customers at reception.

Listening and responding to complaints

Listening is part of communicating, and is especially important when a customer is complaining. Good principles for listening include:

✓ Place yourself and the customer in an appropriate place, possibly away from others.

✓ Avoid distractions – focus on the customer.

✓ Keep an open mind and delay judgement until you have heard everything.

✓ Do not stereotype the speaker, for example by labelling them as a pushy parent.

Respond quickly, but only after you have all the information, so ask for the customer's phone number or email if you need to get back to them. Be polite and balanced, not defensive or negative. Remember: complaints help a business to improve!

Non-verbal communication

This includes:

- body language
- posture
- paralanguage (such as hesitations or pauses during speech)
- personal space
- facial expressions.

These methods are often just as important as speech. Consider how a coach communicates non-verbally, for example over crowd noise or to swimmers whose ears may be filled with water. It is important to be aware of unconscious non-verbal communication, as it can be easily misinterpreted.

Recognising whether customers have special requirements

Do I need to change my language and pitch to suit the age or attention span of the customer?

How can I draw from the differing experiences of men and women and different ethnic backgrounds and situations?

Do I need to change my tone and pitch to help customers who are deaf or hard of hearing?

Considerations for customers who may have special requirements

How can I keep the customer's interest? (For example, be brief and use humour if appropriate.)

Does the customer know the technical words I want to use?

Is my written communication clear enough for the customer to understand?

Now try this

Think about your ideal job in sport. Explain how the way you communicate might have an impact on customers and colleagues. Identify the communication skills you might need.

If you already have a job, consider how you could modify your behaviour to better meet the expectations of others.

Financing a business

Financial statements allow sports businesses to track their financial resources. It is important that the right kind of planning is in place to manage costs so that the business can improve.

Cashflow

Cashflow is perhaps the best indicator of business health. A **cashflow forecast** allows a business to track and predict its **inflow** (income or receipts, the money that comes into a business) and **outflow** (payments or money spent). An inflow greater than outflow suggests good cashflow and a profit. Not having enough money to pay cricket coaches at the end of the month may indicate a poor cashflow and a decline in business.

Fixed costs, variable costs and break even

- **Fixed costs** are not affected by level of sales or output, e.g. salaries, insurance or rent.
- **Variable costs** change depending on sales or output, e.g. a company making footballs buys different amounts of leather, rubber, valves and thread depending on the level of orders.
- **Break even** is the point at which the profits equal the total costs.

Inflows/receipts	Outflows/payments
Cash sales – therapy sessions	Cash purchases – massage oils and towels
Credit sales – client paying at the end of a course of treatments	Credit purchases – not yet paid for, e.g. laundry services
Loans – on the new massage bed	Purchase of assets – car
Capital introduced – investment from partner	Rent for salon
Sale of assets – sold old massage beds	Rates paid to local council
Bank interest received	Wages – paid to cleaner or accountant

Example cashflow for a sports massage therapist

Costs at a tennis centre
Sporting example

Capital costs are usually one-off costs for equipment, land or premises, e.g. buildings and tennis courts.

Operational costs relate to the day-to-day operation of a business, e.g. a racket-stringing machine or refurbishing court surfaces.

Equipment costs might include balls, nets, line paint, office stationery and cleaning fluids. This also includes **upgrading equipment**, for example buying the latest tennis ball machine, nets, fencing or courtside furniture.

Other ways of using financial statements

Here are some other ways of identifying whether a business is developing, improving and making a profit, or declining.

- ✓ **Profit and loss** is a simple statement showing whether a business has made or lost money at the end of the business year.
- ✓ **Balance sheets** give a snapshot of assets (items owned), liabilities (debts and bills) and equity (stock or money invested).
- ✓ **Ratio analysis** compares performance to the last business year or to competitors.

Now try this

You might want to compare your answer with a friend since it is very easy to forget entries on both sides of the forecast.

Design a cashflow template for your personal finances for this month, using the information on this page to help you. Include your opening and closing balances and each source of inflow and outflow. What actions could you take to avoid cashflow issues?

Financial records

Whatever the type of business, it is essential to keep accurate financial records, perhaps with the help of accountants if the business owner or staff lack financial skills. Many types of record are required by law and may be inspected by authorities at short notice.

General legal requirements

All private companies must pay tax based on their profit and loss for the year. They can be fined if their tax return is inaccurate. This means businesses must record all their income and outgoings. Records can be paper, kept on a computer and/or online. VAT-registered and limited companies have additional legal requirements. Limited companies can be fined £3000 or their directors disqualified if they don't keep accounting records.

Self-employed and sole traders

They must keep records of:
- all sales and income
- all business expenses
- tax records
- VAT records (if registered)
- records of personal income.

Records must be kept for at least 5 years after the submission deadline of the tax year.

Other types of records to keep

These may be required as proof of income and outgoings.
- **Sales** – sales books or ledgers, petty cash books, till rolls, invoices and receipts.
- **Purchasing and ordering records** – receipts and details of stock ordered and current stock, record of assets.
- **Financial** – bank statements, bank slips, chequebook stubs.

Limited companies

They must keep records of:
- all sales and income
- all goods they buy and sell and who from/to (unless it's a retail business)
- all business expenses
- tax records
- VAT records
- assets and stock they own
- debts they owe or are owed
- stocktakings used to work out the stock figure.

Records must be kept for at least 6 years after the submission deadline of the tax year.

Wages for employees

If a company has employees, it is also a legal requirement to keep the following records.
- Payroll information like PAYE and income tax deductions.
- Rates of pay.
- Sickness pay and policy.
- Holiday and absence pay.

VAT-registered businesses

As well as general business records, VAT-registered businesses must:
- keep records of all sales and purchases
- keep a VAT account (a summary of the VAT charged on goods and paid on purchases)
- keep all invoices received
- issue and keep copies of VAT invoices
- record non-VAT-reclaimable items such as business entertainment.

Now try this

Explain **five** reasons why it is important for a business to keep accurate financial records.

Trends in the sports and active leisure industry: technology, media and social media

It is important for sports businesses to identify trends and opportunities in the sports and active leisure industry and recognise the associated benefits and risks.

New technologies

New sports technologies provide opportunities for businesses, such as:

- IT in performance analysis and in supporting the officiating of sport
- new materials for optimising performance in clothing, rackets, sailing boats, running shoes or swimming suits
- facilities that are all-weather and environmentally sustainable
- safe, effective training tools like scrum machines in rugby.

Hawk-Eye is a video/computer-based ball-tracking software system widely used in many sports, for example for goal-line technology in football, electronic line-calling in tennis and as a decision-review system in cricket.

Influence of the media

The media enables access to entertainment, information and education. Media traditionally referred to TV, radio and newspapers but now include social media and websites. Online streaming and sites like YouTube are taking over from broadcast content.

The media and sport have a **symbiotic** relationship, where each benefits the other, although there are disadvantages too. The table below gives some examples.

Social media

Social media such as LinkedIn, Instagram, Snapchat and Twitter represent a genuine opportunity for sports businesses to:

- interact with customers at a live event
- see what customers are saying about them
- find new customers
- find potential partners
- customise content for users
- compile personal data that can help target new customers.

The features of the relationship between the media and sport

Advantages for sport	Disadvantages for sport	Advantages for the media	Disadvantages for the media
Spectators willing to pay more to see top performers and build their knowledge	Match attendance figures might fall if there are alternative ways of watching	Subscription fees/ increased sales mean larger profit	Online streaming means that many people do not pay to watch, potentially reducing income
Makes it easier for popular sports to attract sponsorship	Sports stars lose privacy	Sports are attractive, positive brands and add to company credibility	Difficult and expensive to lead in a competitive market
Viewer gets close-up action and instant information	Media force changes to event timings, rules and season dates	Can draw in large amounts of money from advertisers	Subscribers can be fickle so a media company isn't guaranteed loyal customers
Improves participation rates, raises profile and increases popularity of the sport	Media decide what matters, to some extent, e.g. less coverage of women's sports	Can sell other products and services, e.g. pay to view	

Now try this

You could look at LinkedIn, Pinterest, Facebook, Twitter, Instagram, Snapchat and WhatsApp.

Identify two different types of sports business and research how they have used social media to promote their products or services. Explain the advantages and disadvantages to the businesses.

Trends in the sports and active leisure industry: participation and spectator numbers

Traditional sports are, generally, in decline, but it doesn't follow that fewer people are interested in sport. We are spending more time in the gym or pool and less playing rugby or rounders. Sports businesses must adapt to changing trends and participation rates.

Participation rates

According to Full Fact (www.fullfact.org), in 2005–06, 15.6 per cent of adults in England played sport at least three times a week for 30 minutes. By the 2012 London Olympics, this had increased to a peak of 17.7 per cent and has remained at about that level since. However, over the past 10 years there has been a decrease in club membership, sports tuition, and people taking part in competitions and organised sport.

Women's and Paralympic sports are increasing in popularity among both participants and spectators. The internet makes it easier for people to find out about events, classes and leisure centres, lowering a previous barrier to participation.

Sports participation trends 2016

Sport England produces a regular Active People survey (now called Active Lives) that reports on people's activity levels. It reports that 63 per cent of men and 59 per cent of women are active for more than 150 minutes per week. It also suggests that more informal activities like walking, bowls, table tennis and parkour are growing in popularity.

Declining in participation	Increasing in participation
Athletics	Keep fit and gym
Cycling	Football
Rounders	Mountaineering
Squash	Canoeing

Spectator numbers

Almost a quarter (23.5 per cent) of adults say they have attended at least two live sports events in the last 12 months (Active Lives Survey). Attendances at sports events (in terms of tickets sold) were nearly 70 million in 2016, 45.2 million of which were at football matches, including growing numbers at the FA Women's Super League. Tennis, motorsport, golf, horse-racing and equestrian events were also popular. Attendances in 2016 changed little from 2015, with numbers remaining up since the 2012 Olympics, despite the UK hosting fewer international competitions (source: Deloitte). Free events, such as the cycling Tour of Britain, also draw increasing crowds.

Business opportunities

These figures suggest that the sports and active leisure industry offers numerous opportunities for businesses. These include:

- clothes and equipment
- coaching services
- developing new twists on older sports and activities (e.g. mini-trampoline aerobics)
- specialist courses or classes
- event management
- activity-specific advice and information
- providing premises
- merchandise for events and clubs, such as T-shirts or branded water bottles.

Now try this

A growth in participation in adventure sports like paintballing, snowboarding, skateboarding and mountain biking means an increase in demand for related sports businesses. Research the business opportunities offered by one of these activities.

Developing products and services to take advantage of trends

Product development is about taking advantage of trends and trying to improve products or services, whether by designing new products, adapting existing ones or offering new or improved services. It has potential benefits and risks for sports businesses.

Benefits of product development

The main benefits are improvements, diversification and ultimately business growth.

Improving and diversifying products and services – Customers will have a wider choice of products on offer as businesses compete to sell their products, e.g. a football boot manufacturer taking advantage of new lightweight materials, or diversifying by making boots for other sports.

Customer experience – A business that changes its approach to customers can broaden its appeal, e.g. injecting humour into a sports stadium tour, or a personal trainer offering tailored training programmes to individuals.

Development of new target markets – Developing their offering helps businesses to find new customers, perhaps in new areas, e.g. a gym or swimming club developing classes for the parents of child participants.

Benefits

Improved reputation – A business that seeks to improve generally appears more dynamic and responsive, impressing customers and investors.

Offering USPs – A business may develop something that no one else can offer that appeals to a large audience, e.g. a non-leaking water bottle, a new type of exercise class or state-of-the art technology in breathable sports clothing.

Risks of product development

The main risks are wasting time and resources, and overall cost, leading to business decline. Trends come and go so need to be tracked carefully.

Failing to meet customer needs – The business may become so focused on the new idea that the established business is neglected, e.g. reducing provision of the core service of basketball coaching in favour of a basketball clothing line.

Failing to anticipate competitor activities – Being too focused on developing your innovation could stop you from noticing competitors' own developments before customers go to them.

Risks

Failing to achieve a return on investment – Trying new things is always a risk and sometimes that risk doesn't pay off.

Now try this

Research some sports and fitness products or services that interest you and make a product development plan for one by stating ideas about how it could be improved.

> You could start by identifying something that annoys you about training in your sport, and what you could do to improve it.

Your Unit 22 set task

Unit 22 will be assessed through a task, which will be set by Pearson. In this assessed task you will examine the internal and external factors associated with a business and how it may respond to trends affecting business in the sports and active leisure industry.

Revising your skills

Your assessed task could cover any of the essential content in the unit. You can revise the unit content in this Revision Guide. This skills section is designed to **revise the skills** that you might need for your assessed task. The section uses selected content and outcomes to provide an example of ways to apply your skills.

Reviewing the current status of sport businesses (see page 47)

Analysing the internal and external influences (see pages 75 and 76)

Set task skills

Making recommendations (see page 77)

Justifying your recommendations (see page 78)

Workflow

The process of producing a business summary by examining internal and external factors associated with a sports and active leisure business and how it may respond to trends affecting it, might follow these steps:

☑ Research and review sports and active leisure businesses that may be different in size and ownership, considering, for example, facilities, products and services, business operations and demographics.

☑ Read detailed information about businesses and review the current business status, considering central themes such as the purpose of the business.

☑ Use the data to analyse the business model and factors that are currently affecting the business.

☑ Develop recommendations based on marketing, meeting customer and business needs, and matching industry trends.

☑ Justify your recommendations based on the wider sporting context.

Check the Pearson website

The activities and sample response extracts in this section are provided to help you to revise content and skills. Ask your tutor or check the Pearson website for the most up-to-date **Sample Assessment Material** and **Mark Scheme** to get an indication of the structure of your actual assessed task and what this requires of you. The details of the task may change so always make sure you are up to date.

Now try this

Visit the Pearson website and find the page containing the course materials for Unit 22: Investigating Business in the Sport and Active Leisure Industry. Look at the latest Unit 22 Sample Assessment Material for an indication of:

- the structure of your set task, and whether it is divided into parts
- how much time you are allowed for the task, or different parts of the task
- what briefing or stimulus material might be provided
- any notes you might have to make and whether you are allowed to take selected notes into your supervised assessment
- whether you may use a calculator in your supervised assessment
- the activities you are required to complete and how to format your responses.

Getting started with research

If you need to research sports businesses, it is important to know where to look and how to find the specific information and detail that you need.

> Read the task carefully. Notice the number and different types of businesses you need to research. Make sure you carry out research on each of the areas listed.

Task information

Carry out research on three sports and leisure businesses that are different in size and ownership. Your research should include:

- facilities
- products and services
- business operations
- demographics.

> You could start by finding answers to questions like:
> - What is their core message or target market?
> - What is their range and focus for products and/ or services?
> - How do they promote themselves?
>
> Then gather specific information that will help you make comparisons and develop ideas about:
> - internal and external factors
> - the way the business responds to trends affecting the industry.

Reviewing sports businesses

This task brief is used as an example to show the skills you need. Ask your tutor or look at the Sample Assessment Material on the Pearson website to make sure you have the most up-to-date details.

Searching business websites

The most obvious place to start your research is online. Look for the following pages.

- **About** – may range from a simple mission statement to plenty of detail; a good place to start
- **Pricing** – may be available
- **Testimonials** – may indicate the kind of customer and what is important to them
- **Search** – useful for drilling down on specifics, or for anything that you can't find
- **News** – for recent events and successes
- **Shop** – for an idea of the range of products and services

Social media

Most businesses use social media, which is useful for finding up-to-date information and indicates who is interacting with them. You could search:

- ✓ Facebook pages
- ✓ Twitter feeds
- ✓ LinkedIn profiles
- ✓ promotional videos on YouTube
- ✓ photoshares on Instagram
- ✓ others such as Pinterest, Google+, Reddit.

 Links You can revise how businesses use social media on page 65.

In this extract, the size and type of a business is given, as well as its unique selling point.

Data related to the success and growth of the company is also given.

> Sources such as this press release, found during the process of research, can also provide useful information.

PRESS RELEASE

Based in Milton Keynes, the 28-strong Football Whispers team have developed the website and app from concept to two million users per month. Launched to assess the validity of transfer rumours using a unique algorithm, Football Whispers not only ranks transfer rumours with its FW Index, but also powers content for media giants Sky Sports, ESPN and *The Sun*.

Within a year of its official launch, Football Whispers has processed over seven million rumours, from which 9000 transfers have actually completed and over 115000 false positives have been identified. The phenomenal success has already resulted in the website and app winning a Sports Technology Award and making the shortlist for five others, including Sports Business, Drum Marketing on Mobile and DataIQ Talent Awards.

Now try this

Find an example of a sports coaching service online. Using this page as a guide, see what information you can find about its facilities, products and services, business operations and demographics of clients.

> Demographics can be difficult to research, so try the Office for National Statistics (ONS) at www.ons.gov.uk.

Reviewing sources

When researching sports businesses there can be a high volume of information. Here are some examples of skills helpful for identifying useful and relevant information.

Identifying useful content

Look for the following information about a sports business, online or in hard copy.

- Customer demographics – this will indicate what the business will plan to offer, based on factors such as geographical area, age, income, race, gender and education level.

- Description of operations – these provide clarity on what products and services are offered.

- Financial data will indicate the health of the company in the form of cashflow and profit and loss forecasts, as well as balance sheets.

- Business aims or objectives – these help companies focus on survival, growth, profit or increased market share.

- Mission statements – these will show who the business is and why they think customers should buy from them. A mission statement sums up the idea that underpins the business.

- Customer testimonies – these will provide genuine feedback about the performance of a business. Nothing sells more than the endorsement of previous customers, particularly trusted impartial ones.

- Product and service updates – these will demonstrate that a business does not just sit back and take orders, but that it keeps up with trends and responds to changing needs.

- Recent news – this demonstrates that a business wants to stay in touch with its customers.

- How the business markets itself – look out for how a business ensures its reaches its target audience.

Be critical

When reviewing sources, take a critical approach.

✓ Question words like 'best', 'unique' and 'proven' in marketing material. Such language is designed to draw customers, so it may be unfounded.

✓ Scan for facts and figures but check the source is reliable.

✓ Social media gives an up-to-the-minute idea of the company's activities but, again, this is a type of marketing, so may not be totally reliable.

✓ Sometimes it's what the content doesn't say that's significant. For example, if you can't find any financial data, why might this be?

PRESS RELEASE

YouWearMe is the difference you need

YouWearMe has just launched its Slick4 wearable device which claims to be the best performance-tracking device available. It includes better than ever satnav technology that can be streamed with pin-point accuracy to all devices (IOS, PC, etc.)

Dave Newton of Premier League Team Cornwallis United already benefits from YouWearMe and speaks of its many advantages:

"YouWearMe is great. It allows access to instantly available high-quality data and shows trends over time – it's the most useful device I have seen in some time."

YouWearMe has been designed by world-leading sport science experts, taking on board feedback from 17 different sports and over 300 users. Find us on Facebook, Twitter, Instagram and LinkedIn.

Here is an indication of use of social media – a good place to continue your review by checking latest posts and the responses of users.

This extract, found during the process of research, promotes exclusivity of product, but consider whether the marketing content may be exaggerating the claims.

Notice that the technology is endorsed by a credible sports professional. Testimonials add more credibility to the product or service.

 Links Revise promotional techniques on pages 59 and 61.

This suggests the versatility of the product and includes some data about its testers.

If you have researched a sports coaching business on page 69, you could use the information to help your analysis.

Keep asking questions as you read information: why, who, where, what, how?

Now try this

Look again at the information above and analyse it. How reliable are any claims, facts or figures? What other sources could you use to back up this information?

Making notes (1)

When making notes, they need to be clear and contain enough detail to be useful to you. Using bullet points will help you to focus your notes. This page and page 72 provide some guidelines.

Choosing what to write about

- Skim-read your source so that you understand how it is written and whether the information is worth noting!
- Make a note of key features and facts – these could help you create sub-headings to further organise your notes.
- Don't write what you already know, but do write down facts to group later.
- You might want to start your research with a list of subheadings like products and services, prices, and so on, and then leave large gaps to fill.

Making preparatory notes

You may be allowed to take some of your preparatory notes into your supervised assessment. If so, there may be restrictions on the length and type of notes that are allowed. Check with your tutor or look at the most up-to-date **Sample Assessment Material** on the Pearson website for information.

Taking notes

👍 Use bullet points.

👍 Make sure your notes are relevant to the task.

👍 Include key facts and figures from your research.

👎 Don't write pages and pages of notes.

👎 Don't copy large chunks of information from your research.

Command words

When making notes, bear in mind the command words that could appear in your assessment questions:

Justify – Give reasons for the points you are making and how they relate to the task.

Evaluate – Bring together all your information and make a judgement on its relevance.

Analyse – Identify several relevant factors, show how they are linked and explain the importance of each.

Making visual notes

Not everyone thinks or, more importantly, processes thoughts in the same way. You may prefer to take notes in the form of a concept map, mind map or simple spidergram like this one. Spidergrams are more easily remembered by most people, especially if you add colour. They are also great for simplifying a lot of facts and data such as those required for a sports business review.

Evidence also suggests that the action of creating the diagram allows us to make more connections – ones we would not have seen with conventional note-making.

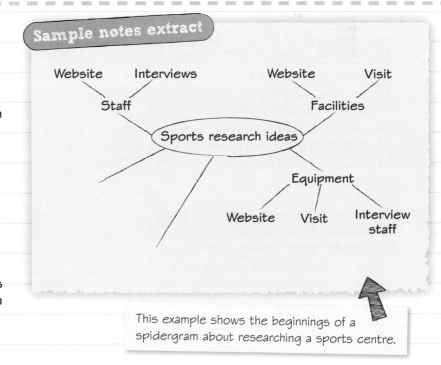

Sample notes extract

This example shows the beginnings of a spidergram about researching a sports centre.

Now try this

Create your own spidergram and, in the centre, write the name of the sports business you plan to research.
Add legs to show the areas you want to research and ideas for possible sources of information.

Making notes (2)

Following on from the guidance on page 71, here is an example of how you can make effective notes from an online source like a company website or a social media profile.

Good-quality use of short-form notes with bullets, which help to keep them concise.

Sample notes extract

Burham Canoe and Kayak Centre

- Based in North Kent with 5 active instructors and 2 admin staff – therefore a micro business.

- Own a small facility with 20 canoes and kayaks, paddles and specialist equipment based in a steel container by the river.

- Have access to changing facilities at an adjoining fitness centre – external factor that could affect business.

- Offer after-school, weekend and holiday activity sessions throughout a season that lasts from March to November – core product/service.

- Sell personal items like waterproofs, spray decks and canoeing footwear – added products to diversify business.

- Established more than 20 years ago by the current director's mother – it's a private-sector business and a sole trader.

- <u>Price structure complicated but essentially individual cost of £10 per two-hour session for under 16 years and £18 for over 16 years</u>

- Membership comes with discount on British Canoe Union membership (legal requirement) and discount on session costs.

- Second small container used to rent private storage for canoes and kayaks and space sold at £30 per space per year – possible business growth opportunity.

Consider the potential focus of your comparison between sports businesses and how your research will help support your ideas.

Note-taking can be in shorthand, e.g. use numerals instead of writing out numbers.

Filter out unnecessary information – decide which facts are most important and which to discard.

Highlight something that you might want to particularly focus on – this fact provides information about cost, discount schemes and business ethos.

Use key phrases, terms or key words like 'cost' or 'price structure'.

Facts and figures are an effective way of providing supporting evidence.

You might find it useful to draw up a checklist of the required topics you need to make notes on. When you have finished your note-taking, go back to the checklist and note any gaps. These will help prompt further research.

Sample notes extract

Checklist
Make notes on:
- ✓ Facilities
- ✓ Products and services
- ✓ Business operations
- ☐ Demographics
- ✓ Purpose of business
- ☐ Identify SWOT or PESTLE factors
- ✓ Business data
- ✓ Customer groups
- ☐ Industry trends
- ☐ Needs of the business

Now try this

Research another canoe and kayak club and make similar notes about it. Compare and contrast it with the example.

You need to identify the key points of both and explain how and why they are similar or different.

Reviewing business information (1)

You may be given further detailed business information as part of your assessment. If so, read it carefully before tackling the activities.

Next Generation Coaching

The business provides canoe and kayak instruction in a medium-sized town with a population of 90 000.

Facilities, products and services

- High-quality training
- Holiday activities
- Lunchtime and after-school coaching
- CPD for teachers

- Equipment and boats provided*
- Links to professional clubs
- Local sports club links

Business operation

- NG operates from the river on the edge of town.
- The business operates in school hours, after school until 5pm and during school holidays.
- The club has no facilities but owns a small van.*
- Income from schools is generated by a direct invoice to schools or the local education authority at a rate of £45 per hour.
- Individual customers pay online at a rate of £18 per day or £75 per week (for holiday courses).
- Other income is priced by arrangement.
- The business is a sole trader – there are two full-time and three part-time members of staff.
- The owner is responsible for HR, staff training and day-to-day management.
- NG communicates offers and schemes with its member schools (22 in the town) via an app, a website and direct email. Advertising is on social media only.

Membership	Price per month	Notes
Junior	£20	Under 16 years
Adult	£40	
Family	£50	Max. 2 boats per family
Concession	£25	

Detailed business information

This extract from task information is used as an example to show the skills you need when reviewing detailed business information. Ask your tutor or check the **Sample Assessment Material** on the Pearson website to find out how many businesses you may need to review and the kind of information you will be given. The content of the set task will be different each year and the details will vary. Each assessment may require different outcomes, so read the brief and activities carefully.

Carefully read through any material that you have been given. Annotate the brief with your own notes and ideas. You could use a symbol or number that corresponds to the category in your own research, for example using underline for business operations, circle for demographics, and asterisks for facilities information.

This is probably the most important piece of information related to a business's current income and may help you make suggestions related to business improvement.

Links Revise demographics and other participation factors on page 47.

Demographics

The town has 90 000 people, 26 primary schools, a professional football team and a large athletics track with which the business does not have links.

AGE	2000	2010	2015
0–5	9433	9054	9341
6–10	9951	10342	10628
11–15	4656	4673	4627
16–20	6478	6549	6572
21–30	11753	11908	11672
41–50	14,582	14059	14349
51–60	12387	12869	12718
61–70	8790	9120	9375
70+	8724	10063	10753
TOTAL	86754	88637	90035

Age-specific demographics help you analyse target markets in terms of trends over time and between different age groups.

You might have researched and made notes on some similar businesses online for comparison.

Now try this

Answer the following questions about the extract above:

1. What are the key advantages of the business in terms of cost and overheads?

2. How could the business exploit social media given that its customers are mostly school children who may not have access to social media?

3. In what way might Next Generation look to expand?

Reviewing business information (2)

If you are asked to review business information, you need to focus on relevant information and interpret it effectively to understand the business's status and factors contributing to its success.

Reviewing and interpreting

For example, when you are reviewing the current business status using the information provided in the task information, consider how you will:

- produce a comprehensive review with reference to the business and sports and active leisure industry
- show detailed understanding of the purpose of the existing business
- show detailed understanding of the data provided in the given scenario
- show detailed use of research from the sports and active leisure industry, using examples to support the review of the scenario.

Using your preparatory research

When writing your review, make use of information that you have researched about businesses. Here are examples of points you could include:

✓ Trends in similar businesses.

✓ Similarities or differences to businesses you have researched.

You could also consider additional products and services that could improve the business:

✓ Strengths and weaknesses.

✓ Factors affecting the business.

✓ The main aim of the business.

✓ Conclusions you can draw from current business data.

Sample response extract

The business is a private company that provides sports coaching in primary schools. It is a small business and its main aims are to make a profit and offer a good service.

The business offers programmes that promote fitness and participation to the whole community.

The main customers are school children but also teachers who require qualified sports coaches to deliver a range of sports.

Stakeholders are not involved in this business as it is owned and managed by one person who recruits all the staff.

The company must comply with safeguarding and data protection legislation as well as be aware of the health and safety requirements of each activity.

This extract from a learner's sample review refers to the revision task information on page 73. It could include more information about the scope of the business (local) and the fact sample that employing fewer than nine members of staff makes it a microbusiness.

Say as much as you can about the aims and objectives of the business to demonstrate that you understand the purpose of the business. This sample answer could expand on this aspect.

This part of the sample answer is not correct as stakeholders include customers, staff and external influences such as competitors and, in this case, other school departments and play associations.

This response does provide clear evidence for the current status of the business, and an understanding of the nature of the existing business.

Now try this

Continue to review the business, including a conclusion summing up how successful you think it is, given the information you have and your additional knowledge.

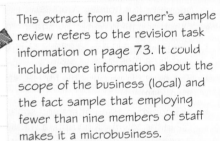

Look back at the information about Next Generation Coaching on page 73 to help you.

Business model analysis: SWOT

You may be asked to use the PESTLE or SWOT methods to analyse the business model and factors that are currently affecting a business. Use your analysis to help you evaluate the internal and external factors relating to a business, and to understand their impact on its development. In this extract from a learner response, the SWOT analysis is being applied to Next Generation Coaching.

Business models

A business model is a plan for effective operation, and considers income sources, client base and the products and services offered. Any **analysis** of a business model will need to consider how effectively the business uses its status as well as comparing competitor activity. This sample response extract is presented in a simple SWOT framework. Your analysis should use the SWOT model for evaluation, supported with examples, drawing on wider research.

Links Revise SWOT analysis on page 51.

Sample response extract

Strengths
- Steady income from reliable school sources.
- Location by the river perfect for canoeing.
- Good use of social media for business communication.

Weaknesses
- No time spent researching potential investors.
- Lack of facilities makes equipment storage a challenge and generally limited to van (security issue).
- IT infrastructure is small scale and dependent upon skills of owner.

This answer has highlighted that income is the most important factor for any business.

Consider current trends in the industry. Here the use of social media is identified as a strength, as a free and useful source of personal data and promotional opportunities.

While facilities can be an advantage, here there is a consideration of the financial burden they can present.

This answer has identified outsourcing as an opportunity, weighing up the cost against the potential advantages.

Here, a potential free source of workers has been highlighted. These motivated volunteers could be valuable, free assistant coaches. They could also be a way to recruit new paid members of staff.

Consideration is given here to how government policy and funding for PE provision can change. Currently, the business benefits from primary schools being able to design and fund their own programmes, but this policy could change.

Look at competitor activity to identify any threats to the business. Other businesses cannot be stopped from offering similar services and products, and it helps a business to keep a close eye on them and constantly review their offer.

Sample response extract

Opportunities
- Consider outsourcing HR tasks such as salary management and staff recruitment.
- New technology, such as video analysis, can be adapted to sports coaching.
- Potential volunteer workforce from local college (sports leaders)
- Expansion of non-school business
- Slight rise in recent years of most age groups in the town

Threats
- Political changes to the way that PE is delivered, e.g. could be change in what can be taught and how it is assessed
- Cuts to school funding
- Local rival businesses taking clients
- Environmental legislation, e.g. river authority charges/canoeing licences

Now try this

Research how a volunteer strategy could provide opportunities and threats for a business like Next Generation.

You might start by searching on the Sport England website for information that explores volunteering.

Business model analysis: PESTLE

Applying business model analysis, using methods such as SWOT and PESTLE, can help you evaluate the internal and external factors relating to a business, and to understand their impact on its development. In this extract from a learner response, a PESTLE analysis is being applied to look at Next Generation Coaching. This extract presents a simple PESTLE framework. Your analysis should be supported with examples, drawing on wider research.

This extract from a response considers how pollution could be disastrous for a river-based coaching business, which should take out insurance against not being able to use the river.

The state of the national economy is a continual external factor in a business's success. This answer has highlighted the difficult economic environment. In such an environment, non-essential expenses are the first to suffer and many clients would consider sports coaching to be non-essential.

This answer has identified how, in a competitive market, where customers have options, businesses must offer good value and maintain a dialogue with customers, listening to their ideas.

Sample response extract

Political
- Ecological/legislative issues related to the river, e.g. pollution.
- The cost of registering with bodies such as the Adventure Activities Licensing Authority (AALA).
- Awareness of small business grants/loans.

Economic
- UK economy, e.g. recession, boom.
- Local economic factors such as Local Education Authority (LEA) funding.

Social
- Demographics, e.g. age sectors that are in decline or on the rise.
- Pressure on customer service.
- Need to satisfy value for customers.
- Increasing age and other trends, e.g. obesity.

Technological
- Use of apps and social media encourage a strong brand identity in local schools.

Legal
- Changes in laws related to safeguarding of children and data protection.

Environmental
- Cost of Environment Agency river-use licences

 Links Revise PESTLE analysis on pages 52 and 53.

Here, it is identified that membership of regulatory bodies demonstrates a responsible business, and will help develop a good reputation.

Here, demographics have been identified as indicators of future business. Products and services could be aimed at the fastest expanding age category to increase the target market.

More demographical trends have been highlighted here. It is vital that businesses stay aware of social trends (e.g. Next Generation could improve its offering to the over-50s or offer after-5pm classes to enable families to participate in social sessions).

This answer identifies a specific environment-related cost to the business. A range of recent legal changes concern protecting the environment, so it is worth watching the new policies of key organisations like the Environment Agency for the potential impact such policies have on the business.

What issues can the business influence?

A PESTLE analysis allows you to focus on both internal aspects (which the business can control) and external aspects (which the business can't control). The same process can be applied to competitors for comparison.

Now try this

Look at the following characteristics of a business analysis. Rank them in order of significance for Next Generation Coaching and justify your decision. (There is no one right answer.)

- The need to train staff
- Dealing with competitors
- Managing cashflow
- Investing in facilities
- Seeking financial backing/partners
- Investigating new niche markets and income streams

Making recommendations

If asked to recommend how a sports and active leisure business can develop and market itself, you need to consider customer groups, trends in the industry and the needs of the business. This will involve you in understanding a sports business's current status and how the business can adapt. You should give detailed examples to support your recommendations. Here is some guidance on the skills involved, using Next Generation Coaching as an example.

Sample response extract

Recommendations for Next Generation Coaching:

1. Increase lunchtime sports offering.
2. Offer new popular activities like cheerleading, yoga and martial arts.
3. Offer staff a set number of training courses per year.
4. Recruit more staff and increase offer.
5. Consider investment in low-cost facilities for canoeing part of the business, e.g. steel storage container.
6. For some sports, develop exit routes to established and professional clubs.
7. Have 'gifted and talented' clubs to support skill development and support primary-school teaching staff.
8. Engage target markets (e.g. girls' sports, disability sports) more effectively, and take advantage of the funding available.
9. Consider outsourcing IT and HR so that the focus of key staff is on the core business.
10. Improve marketing and technology strategy by outsourcing both.

This demonstrates that you understand trends – not just the latest craze but activities that are proven to be growing in popularity and represent genuine business opportunities.

 Links Revise trends on pages 65 and 66.

This shows an understanding of how staff can be best used to benefit the business.

 Links Revise human resources on page 56.

This shows that a recommendation has been considered for the most talented and keen, and demonstrates an awareness of the credibility gained by having links with other organisations.

This recommendation demonstrates an awareness of current government policy and helps argue for a coherent and structured process.

Links Political influence is part of a PESTLE analysis, which you can revise on page 52.

It is important that your recommendations are **coherent** (clear and structured) and consider the development needs of the business, using specific examples, as this response has done.

This demonstrates an understanding of how using cloud-based systems for project management, accounting and customer relationship management (CRM) would benefit the business and provide a professional corporate image. Many companies offer such services so a price may be negotiated within budget.

Look back again at page 73 to remind yourself of the demographic data provided for Next Generation.

Now try this

Research archery tag and, using the same demographic data as for Next Generation, make recommendations on how a sole trader can improve their business.

Justifying your recommendations

You will need to justify any recommendations you make. Here are some examples of skills involved, using Next Generation Coaching as an example.

Justifying

When writing your justification, make sure that you link it to the recommendations you have made. Bring together your ideas, providing evidence and giving a strong argument for why they should be implemented. Your justifications should make comprehensive links between businesses and the **wider business context**, supported by examples. This might include factors such as business growth, target markets, risks and trends.

Sample response extract

1. **Increase lunchtime sports offering** – This would be a quiet time for school provision so targeting local workers' lunch hours maximises the available hours for generating an income. This means the business is not as dependent on a single market (schools).

   This shows an awareness of ways to increase and diversify the target market.

2. **Offer new popular activities like cheerleading, yoga and martial arts** – This increases income streams by providing a wider choice of activities, by diversifying and tapping into the target market's current interests. Extending the range of services also offers additional employment opportunities, widens the target market and improves the business's reputation.

   It is a good idea to use relevant terms such as 'income streams', 'diversifying' and 'target market'. This response considers the wider impact of offering new services, although it could also consider the risks of diversifying.

3. **Offer staff a set number of training courses per year** – Allowing staff to grow and gain new skills is both beneficial to them and will help with wider issues such as customer service, since not all training needs to be coaching-related. Knowledgeable staff will also help to improve internal processes.

   This considers the internal and external benefits of training staff. Again, the answer could consider risks such as skilled staff leaving for more senior jobs elsewhere.

4. **Recruit more staff and increase offer** – Investing in more staff with new, specialist skills should provide a payback in terms of being able to run additional classes covering new activities, which should attract new customers and raise income.

   This demonstrates an awareness that while paying for more staff is a cost, it is also an investment as the income may eventually outweigh the expenditure.

5. **Consider investment in low-cost facilities** – This type of business does not need extensive facilities but it is important to have somewhere secure to store equipment.

   As the business currently stands, a steel storage container is a good, low-budget idea for securely storing equipment. However, this answer could be extended to cover facilities that may be necessary if the business offers the types of class suggested if it expands; for example, would it need to hire a sports hall to provide cheerleading or martial arts activities?

Now try this

Continue to provide justifications for the remaining recommendations on the previous page.

Answers

Unit 19: Development and Provision of Sport and Physical Activity

1. Participation
1 Love of the sport/enjoyment/to give something back.
2 *Learner response.*

2. Inclusivity
1 For example, Sport England's 'Start, Stay, Succeed' in sport campaign.

3. Progression along the sports development continuum
1 High levels of knowledge, including tactical.
2 *Learner response.*

4. Gender, age and socio-economic barriers
1 *Learner response.*
2 Tennis, water polo, equestrian, show jumping.

5. Ethnicity and disability barriers
1 *Learner response.*
2 *Learner response.*

6. Solutions to barriers (1)
1 (a) *Learner response.*
  (b) *Learner response.*
2 *Learner response.*
3 *Learner response.*

7. Solutions to barriers (2)
Learner response, suggested answers:
Many sports are perceived as being expensive, therefore not accessible for mass participation.
Tennis can be seen as a game for the middle and upper classes. Court hire, equipment and club membership fees can be costly. However, the Lawn Tennis Association (LTA) has developed many initiatives to try and overcome these barriers, for example: introducing tennis to schools in a fun and interactive way, setting up free/subsidised tennis in local park courts, and working with tennis clubs to make them more player-friendly.
Golf is another sport that can be viewed as elitist and expensive. Similar to tennis, the purchase of the correct equipment, golf course hire fees and club membership can be major barriers to participation. The national governing body (NGB) for golf, England Golf, has developed an initiative called 'Get into Golf' which is designed to make the sport accessible by working with clubs to offer low-cost activities.
Sailing and other water sports can also be costly to participants. Although the NGB – the Royal Yacht Association (RYA) – has developed inclusive programmes and opportunities to increase participation, unless individuals live near or have access to water, the chance of them experiencing the sport is slim. Therefore, the RYA could develop and introduce dry-land sailing initiatives that are accessible for schools and communities to utilise, and perhaps offer groups the opportunity to have free/subsided in taster sessions.

8. Impact on community cohesion and health
1 *Learner response.*
2 *Learner response.*

9. Impact on regeneration, crime and education
Learner response,
Examples could include: Rio 2016 Olympics, Delhi 2010 Commonwealth Games.
The community in Rio has benefited in several ways from the 2016 Olympics. Many jobs were created and the base of the social pyramid in Rio mostly benefited from the increase in labour income during the pre-Olympic period.
In addition, a recent study concluded that the seven years prior to the Games (the decision to host the Games had been taken before this seven-year period) brought more progress than the previous period in areas such as public services, education, health and social development.
Communities have also seen improvements in the provision of services and opportunities, with legacy facilities now open to the community so they can enjoy and play sports, leading to healthier active lifestyles of residents.

10. Local stakeholders
Netball exemplar:
- Local level – potential players, local authority, facilities owners, sports development officer, local businesses for sponsorship.
- National level – England Netball, government (for grants).

11. National- and global-level stakeholders
For example:
1 Athletics – NGB is Athletics UK
2 Aims – win more medals to inspire the public; stage great events to engage the public; increase participation to build an athletic nation; host the best ever World Championship to make the country proud.

12. Stakeholder functions
Learner response (no one correct answer, but a strong answer will justify reasoning).

13. Key stakeholder personnel
1 Yes. For example, a participant may also have a role in the club such as being an administrator.
2 An advantage would be that the person is heavily involved in the club so wants to see the club developing and moving forward. A disadvantage would be that because the person is heavily involved in the club they may want things completed/accessed in a particular way. It may be better to have different input in driving the initiative/club forward.

14. Purpose of measuring sports development
1 Aims must be SMART for a number of reasons:
  - S – specific to the aims and objectives of the club; without this, the club/facility or individual may not be able to meet specific targets.
  - M – measurable; the development must be able to be measured so it can be rated on its success.
  - A – achievable; the initiative, or targets must be achievable or it is pointless setting targets.

- R – realistic; must be realistic in what it is setting out to achieve.
- T – time-constrained; there is a timeframe for when the sport development initiative is delivered/completed.

2 *Learner response*, but good examples are the websites of the NGBs and Sport England.

15. Methods of measuring sports development

1 Benchmarking: An advantage is that agencies are in control of setting their own targets, therefore are in a better position to measure whether the development or initiative is SMART to begin with. A disadvantage is that continuous monitoring and evaluating could be detrimental to employees as they feel they are constantly being 'checked' on.
Quality scheme: An advantage is that an initiative can be measured quickly and with support from agencies such as Sport England. A disadvantage is that the percentage system may not always be accurate if you fall between categories.
Key performance indicators: An advantage is that it is clear very quickly how well a goal has been achieved. A disadvantage is that constant monitoring and evaluation for employees may make them feel under pressure.
Data and research: An advantage is that data and research are cost-effective and easily accessed. A disadvantage is that evidence may not always show what you want it to.

2 *Learner response.*

16. Wider impact when hosting an event

1 International events may require new infrastructure which will have environmental and economic impacts which need to fit in with government policy. The government will need to balance all needs and work with various stakeholders to deliver large international events. The investment needed for a such an event may be beyond what one particular organisation can provide so the government may need to supply the funding.

2 Governments like to play a part in major national and international events as the events showcase the country. They want to be seen in the best light around the world so others form a positive image of the country.

17. Wider impact of implementing an initiative or scheme

1 *Learner response.*
2 *Learner response*, examples could include Sky Living for Sport/Active Playgrounds/Leadership Awards, such as Sports Leaders Awards.

18. Wider impact of developing a facility or club

1 *Learner response* (see Sport England scenarios for information in most areas).
2 Sometimes stakeholders do not have the funds or money to invest in this, and other developments in the area may encompass the facility. The local authority may not, therefore, want to waste money investing in something that may eventually be knocked down.

19. Different types of media (1)

1 Disadvantages:
- TV and satellite – Not everyone has access to satellite as this can be expensive and is therefore is not inclusive to all.
- Social network sites – Information is not always accurate as anyone can post (on open access sites).

Solutions:
- TV and satellite – You could enable sporting events such as football leagues to be televised through accessible channels (this is however unlikely to happen due to owing the amount of money involved in selling the rights).
- Social network sites – Organisations need to actively remove negative or incorrect information.

20. Different types of media (2)

1 Companies, teams and athletes cannot always control how they are reported in the media. For example, positive news about them may be ignored and negative news and scandals may be extensively reported.
2 *Learner reponse.*

21. Use of media in sport

Advantages include that if the athlete is at the peak of their career and performing well, they can gain many endorsements and sponsorship deals, especially if they are representing their country on a national or international scale (e.g. Euro 2016). Disadvantages include that if the athlete does not perform, or if they are involved in some type of scandal, the media can demonise them or their performance. This can lead to a loss of sponsorship which in turn can lead to a huge loss of earnings or endorsements, which is seen on a national or international scale. Other negatives can include invasion of privacy (e.g. photos taken on holiday/family time).

22. Sustainable commercialisation: funding sources

1 They have targets to meet, such as ensuring there are enough people active in the community/enough opportunities to allow people to take part in the sport. Also aids with more uptake in the sport because if the facilities are available people will use them.
2 Businesses such as supermarkets can improve their reputation, so that more people shop at their stores.

23. Sustainable commercialisation: budgeting

Learner response.

24. Sustainable commercialisation: distribution of funds

If they don't adhere to their budgets, there is a risk of agencies being in debt or overspending and this will threaten the initiative or scheme.

25. Ethics of commercialisation

1 *Learner response.* For example, the beer brand Heineken sponsoring the 2019 Rugby World Cup.
2 Companies do this to advertise their brand. This means that millions of people around the world will see their logo and associate it positively with the event, building their reputation. Companies tend to want to be associated with winning.

26. Impact of the media and commercialisation

Learner response.

27. Proposal writing

Learner response, but should include several authoritative sources, for example information from NGB websites or from local authorities.

28. Proposal structure

1 and 2 *Learner response*, but must include valid evidence.

29. Timeframe, costs and resources

If costs escalate there is a threat the country will overspend and then be in debt, and the Games may be threatened.
This is detrimental to the country as they will have to repay this debt back for many years. It will also be bad for their international reputation and they may not be selected to host a prestigious event again.

30. Interrelationship between proposals and the wider context

Examples of ways in which stakeholders could benefit are via: increased publicity, public awareness of their brand, mutually beneficial outcomes (for example, the police want to see the reduction in crime too), and the increased health of the community which will benefit all parties.

31. Your Unit 19 set task

Learner response.

32. Task information and research sources

- Similarities – Both campaigns are aimed at engaging adults in their sport in a fun and sociable environment. They are pitched at adults who either haven't played the sport for a while or are complete novices. Both initiatives are run and funded via their respective NGBs and both are usually delivered by clubs of that sport.
- Differences – 'Back to Netball' is targeted at women, whereas 'Back to Hockey' is for both men and women. The 'Back to Netball' programme is all year round, while 'Back to Hockey' tends to focus on a particular weekly campaign/initiative.

33. Reading and interpreting research

Both projects have seen an increase in participation, with a significant number of participants transitioning into the mainstream club sessions. This could bring about an increase in lifelong participation, therefore contributing towards wider health benefits.

34. Making notes

Aim:
To attract people back to the sport who haven't played it for a while, increasing participation in hockey.
Wider impact on clubs who have taken on the programme:
- An increase in club players
- An increase in casual players
- Additional income for the clubs
- Extra publicity for the club
- New volunteering opportunities to develop and widen the workforce

Wider impact on the participants:
- Development of 'feel-good factor' among players – bringing about improved health and well-being
- Opportunity to create new friendships and forge social cohesion
- Opportunity to increase fitness, learn new skills and play team hockey in a fun and sociable environment

35. Reviewing further information

Without the club having its own base, it is reliant on the facilities of other organisations and partners. This can have implications on the ability to deliver sessions, and therefore on participation.
Possible problems/threats:
- Seasonal/weather: Owing to poor weather in winter months, the club relies on the use of a school's hall, which not only has cost implications, but is also likely to be a shared-use facility. For example, schools often need their hall for their own fixtures and events, stopping clubs from being able to use it, which can have a negative impact on the ability to train.

- Conditions: the poor condition of two of the courts limits the club's capacity and its ability to take on new participants. The club may have to cap the number of players that can play at any one time.

Ways to overcome barriers:
- Many clubs who use or hire a school's facilities often have partnership agreements in place, enabling them to use the facility for free in exchange for a certain number of free places for pupils, staff or parents. This is a useful way of saving money and increasing participation, enabling the club to invest any funding or income generated into new equipment and coaching, together with training fees.
- It may be feasible to find a new facility with adequate courts, perhaps at another school. Many schools are open to allowing clubs to use their facilities, as part of the government's 'Use of School' initiative.

36. Planning a proposal

Aims – to encourage people back to playing hockey by developing their skills with four, one-hour skills sessions, once a week for four weeks. Aim to have ten people per session.
Performance indicators – maintain a register of the number of participants who come to each session and how many attend all four.
Activity – skills sessions focusing on basic hockey moves and rules of the game.
Resources – one coach needed per session; one pitch or indoor space needed (local club facilities, or school facilities if club is busy); no kit provided; cost of hiring the facility and coach's time to be covered by charging £5 per participant.
Interrelationship to sports development – participants can improve their health through physical activity and have the opportunity to make friends and bring the community together. It is hoped that participants will go on to become members of the local club and progress to competitive sport.

37. Writing about aims

The aim of the initiative is to encourage people back to hockey by developing a 'Back to Hockey' scheme, designed to enable men and women to focus on fun, fitness and friendship. The initiative will provide participants with an opportunity to get fit, learn new skills and play team hockey in a fun and sociable environment.
This falls in line with England Hockey's focus on developing the game and offering a more flexible offer for players, for example by including more summer sessions at times to suit demand.
England Hockey's capability of meeting the targets set by Sport England determines the investment that Sport England provides the NGB. England Hockey's measures demonstrate that there are now more people playing hockey than before the 2012 Olympics, with the success of the women's 2016 Olympic gold-medal-winning team having increased awareness of, and exposure to, the sport.

38. Writing about performance indicators

Possible performance indicators could be:
- to see 10 participants at each session
- to see 75 per cent of those 10 participants attend 4 sessions = 7 (this is also known as the retention figure).

Other answers are acceptable as long as the performance measures are:
- clearly linked to aims
- measurable
- linked to current research
- linked to potential impact.

39. Writing about activities

Possible answer:

- Who – qualified female coach who is suitable for target group (appropriate qualifications/experience and rapport) will be employed to deliver 'Back to Hockey' sessions, lasting 1 hour per session (one session per week) for four consecutive weeks.
- What – coach will deliver skills sessions focusing on basic hockey moves and rules of the game.
- Why – to introduce the sport in a fun and engaging way, with the aim of building up participants' confidence and competence to play in a competitive game.
- Where – using one court at the local club's facility.

40. Writing about resources

Possible answer:

- Financial – cost of hiring the facility and coach's time to be covered by a charge of £5 per participant.
- Physical – one pitch or indoor space needed (local club facilities, or school facilities if club is busy), balls and netball posts.
- Human resources – one coach needed per session, plus administrator to carry out paperwork, e.g. take bookings and process registration.

41. Writing about wider sports development

1 The 'Back to Hockey' proposal will make hockey more accessible by providing opportunities to local women to get back into the sport. Using local facilities and keeping the cost of participating low will help ensure the league is accessible to local people from a variety of socio-economic backgrounds. The league will be advertised locally and nationally, thus helping make hockey a more visible sport.
2 Possible answer:
   - Environmental – a healthier and fitter nation improves the wider environment. However, greater participation will lead to an increased need for facilities, therefore creating the potential for new facility development which can have an impact on the carbon footprint and wider environment.
   - Political – the current political landscape and emphasis given to sport can affect the level of funding invested in particular sports. Sport England will invest in sports whose Whole Sport Plans can demonstrate how they are going to raise the profile of the sport and meet specific targets. The results achieved at major sporting events (for example, number of medals won at an Olympics) can also have an impact on the level of funding allocated to each sport.
   - Cultural and/or economic – although it is played in many state schools, hockey has traditionally been seen as a private-school, inaccessible sport. Therefore, people from lower socio-economic backgrounds may not perceive hockey as appropriate for them. This proposal can therefore help address these stereotypes, making the sport more accessible.

Unit 22: Investigating Business in the Sport and Active Leisure Industry

42. Types of sports and active leisure businesses

Possible answer:

- Sports Direct International is a plc. It is a large company that operates across the world, controlling many well-known brands, with a revenue of nearly £3 billion. Its status enables it to spread the financial risk across a number of divisions, as well as offering opportunities to grow further. A 'plc' status is also prestigious, which can lead to greater brand recognition and more sales.
- Barcelona FC is a cooperative sporting association. More than 175 000 people pay an annual fee to be a member, and they all have a say in how the club is run. This brings in a large income that enables the club to develop, as well as allowing it to invest in local sports community programmes. Owing to the fact that they can influence the club's financial and promotion decisions, members are more invested in the success of the club than ordinary fans.
- Freedom Leisure is both a limited company and a charitable trust. It is not-for-profit and its aim is to invest in improving the health and well-being of local communities.
- Aspire Sports is a limited company. It offers localised sports coaching services and events to schools, organisations and individuals for a profit but it also has a charitable arm, Aspire Sports Trust, that helps to promote sport in the community.

43. Scope and size of business activities

Learner response. Your answer needs to clearly differentiate between the different types and sizes of business. Examples may be local, national or international.

44. Aims and objectives of the private sector

Learner response. Your answer needs to clearly differentiate between different types and sizes of business. Examples may be local, national or international.

45. Aims and objectives of the public and voluntary sectors

Learner response. You must ensure that all objectives are SMART and consider the criteria for success in the table on page 45. Your examples should emphasise criteria such as value for money and controlling costs over profit.

46. Provision of services and their purpose

Learner response. Your answer should take into account:

- the times they can attend – likely to be before and after work, and at lunchtime. The gym may need to encourage retired people or learners to use the facilities during work hours in order to make the business cost-effective.
- suitable one-to-one programmes/types of activities – office workers are likely to be sedentary for most of the day so activities could address the issues associated with this, e.g. weight gain, back and shoulder pain, lack of muscle tone. Members may want cardio classes or programmes to make up for this. They may also want stretching activities, such as yoga or Pilates, or weight training. Activities and classes should be interesting and engaging, so that members will attend despite the stresses of their working day. Massages and nutritional advice may also be popular.
- how to encourage regular members

Your answer should take into account: the gym cannot depend on just proximity to the office if there are similar facilities nearby. Options include offering other services, such as refreshments, which may be an option if there is space, or promotions such as discounts for those working in the office above, or reduced car-parking charges during the day.

47. Customer groups: demographics and purpose

Learner response. Your answer could include:
- apps to help plan and control water and dietary requirements, such as meal plans to break the fast
- apps to help plan and time suitable workouts when water cannot be drunk
- customised personal training
- advice and consultancy to help plan in advance, e.g. accepting that training and diet will be different during this time, or getting the body's metabolism used to intermittent fasting before Ramadan begins.

48. Meeting customer needs

Learner response. Your answer should take into account the general principles of effective yet ethical sales techniques. For example:
- Listen to the customer, find out a little about their exercise history and why they want to join the gym, and address their concerns and particular circumstances.
- Personalise your response to the customer. If you give them a tour, show them the facilities and services that would interest them most.
- Suggest membership options that best match the customer's requirements, not just the most expensive ones, e.g. if they tell you they have childcare responsibilities in the evenings, don't suggest a membership that includes evening classes.
- Be friendly, approachable and sincere – people buy from people they like.
- Find out as much as possible about the gym's facilities and services, so that you can confidently answer questions.
- Also find out as much as possible about competing gyms, and identify what makes your gym a better choice (without criticising the competitors).
- Be clear and transparent about the legal restrictions and requirements, such as a cooling-off period.
- Prepare a loose script or plan so that you know how you will guide the discussion beforehand – but also remain flexible so you can address the customer's needs.

49. Stakeholders

Stakeholders could include:
- internal stakeholders – managers, owners, staff (e.g. reception, administrators, trained instructors)
- external stakeholders – suppliers, competitors, creditors, customers (could be of all ages so also need to consider parents or guardians of children), interest groups, trade associations, land owner.

50. Laws, legislation and safeguarding

Learner response. Your answer should include the following considerations:
- legal requirements
- first-aid arrangements
- rules for safe jumping, e.g. only one person on a trampoline at a time; land on two feet; do not run; no double flips; obey staff instructions or interventions
- mandatory participant information and safety videos
- mandatory visitor warm-ups
- special requirements for children and disabled people
- staff training
- risk assessment
- disclaimer forms and data protection
- actions to take if customers engage in unsafe practices.

51. Business models: SWOT analysis

Learner response. Your answer should be based on a SWOT template and use realistic factors. Examples could include:

Strengths
- Expertise – You can offer a high level of training knowledge, including in anatomy and physiology, aqua fitness and in teaching children.
- Customer need – There are few private opportunities for children to learn to swim out of school, and parents are willing to pay for private or small-group lessons. There are also no aqua- fitness classes available for adults.

Weaknesses
- No marketing budget – There may be difficulty in breaking into the new market because of the cost of producing flyers, setting up a website, etc.
- No local contacts – Being new to the area means that a network of facilities managers and clients needs to be built from scratch.

Opportunities
- Untapped market – There are few private opportunities for children to learn to swim out of school, and parents are willing to pay for private or small-group lessons.
- Low competition – There are few other swimming coaches locally and the market is large.
- Partnerships – Establishing partnerships with local swimming pools will create revenue for both them and you.

Threats
- Competition – Swimming pools may offer lessons themselves if they see there is a market for it.
- Pricing – Increased competition is likely to push prices down over time.

52. Business models: PESTLE analysis (1)

1 Possible threats – It might take customers away from the fitness centre because they are participating in team sports instead.
2 Possible opportunities – The fitness centre could partner with the local authority to offer team sports on site, for both adults and children.

53. Business models: PESTLE analysis (2)

Learner response. Your answer could include the following:
P – equality and diversity, DBS checks, health and safety
E – club funding, sport (NGB) funding, collecting subscriptions
S – culture balance, religion, media, social media
T – promotions and marketing, advertising, social media
L – Health and Safety at Work Act, NGB, data protection, safe-working practices
E – carbon footprint, responsible use of facilities, energy consumption.

54. Job roles and person specifications

Learner response. Remember to make your action plan SMART.

55. Types of employment

Learner response. Your answer should include a clear justification for why the chosen opportunities appeal. Examples could include:
- Flexible hours enable the work to fit around college and hobbies.
- The on-the-job training provides valuable experience, and perhaps a qualification, for future paid jobs.
- Opportunity is close by, which makes it easy to get to and reduces commuting time.
- It offers the chance to work with in chosen field to find out whether it's worth pursuing as a career.
- Chance to help others to develop their skills and interest will be satisfying.

- There may be additional benefits, e.g. every hour spent tutoring beginners on a dry ski slope may be repaid with a free hour of skiing later.

56. Human resource management

Possible answer:

People who are new to the industry are likely to be paid less than those with more experience, unless they have useful transferable skills such as management. A leisure centre assistant in their first job may earn about £10000 a year, or near to the minimum wage at an hourly rate, but over time this is likely to rise. Leisure centre managers may earn £26000 or more, but they will have additional responsibilities such as financial management, team management and dealing with customer complaints.

Salaries may be higher in the private sector than the public sector. For example, sports development officers for a local authority may earn less than £20000 per year, whereas programme managers for large sports organisations may earn up to £40000. Those with specialist skills and relevant academic or practical qualifications will be more in demand and can usually command a higher salary. For example, sports scientists in a niche sector can expect to earn £35000, or significantly more at the highest levels of competitive sport.

Sole traders, such as coaches or personal traders, may charge clients by the hour or for a set contracted amount if they work with a school or leisure centre. However, they must pay for their overheads, tax and other business expenses from their income. Professional sportspeople will need to ensure their income (from pay and sponsorship) is sufficient to maintain a standard of living. Only those very few who are among the best in the world can expect to earn millions, or even hundreds of thousands. Professional footballers are an exception but, again, there is huge competition for these jobs and only the best and most fortunate will become rich.

57. Physical resources: planning and maintenance

Learner response. Your answer should take into account:
- limited budget
- supplies and materials
- staffing
- risk control
- emergency cover
- health and safety
- assets
- leasing options
- maintenance and refurbishment.

Costs should be realistic and consider the priorities when sticking to a budget.

58. Importance of resource management

Possible answer: JSC Sports Coaching is likely to need:
- appropriate training for staff so that they can deliver a range of sports coaching
- contracts in place for staff, outlining pay and hours
- suitable venues hired across the area
- marketing and promotional items and activities organised and distributed in good time before the holidays
- an easy booking process, such as online using Paypal
- availability to answer parents' questions
- equipment such as balls or mats, or to have equipment available at venues
- transport such as a van, especially if staff are supplying their own equipment
- administration in place, such as a health and safety policy, a waste reduction plan, risk assessments and DBS checks
- a clear financial plan, including how many courses/participants are needed to make a profit while staying within a realistic capacity.

59. Marketing: 7 Ps (1)

Learner responses, taking into account the Ps covered on both pages. The responses could take into account:

Product
- Product life cycles
- Unique selling points (USPs)
- Product range
- Meeting customer needs

Promotion
- Above the line (mass media: TV, newspaper advertising, digital, social media)
- Below the line promotion (specific, memorable methods focused on groups of customers, e.g. direct marketing via letter, email or targeted leaflet drop
- Target market
- Brand image
- Celebrity endorsements

Price
- Pricing strategies
- Promotional discounts

Place
- Convenience to customer
- Timing, e.g. tying in promotion with an important tournament

People
- Customer service
- Relationship between people and brand image

Process
- Managing customer interactions consistently
- Tying in with lifestyle choices, e.g. current nutritional research or guidelines or social aspect of the product or service

Physical environment
- Reflecting brand image in a physical environment
- Appropriateness to offering, e.g. being able to clearly see what is being bought
- Creating a good impression

60. Marketing: 7 Ps (2)

Refer to answer to page 59.

61. Customer services and meeting customer needs

Learner response. Your customer care policy should include:
- the required level of knowledge for chosen role, e.g. covering types of classes, times, locations, age ranges, costs, size of group, clothing required, facilities and equipment available, waiting lists.
- what to do if answers are not known immediately, e.g. take customer's details and ask manager or coach, getting back to customer within 48 hours
- benefits for the customer, including promotions, e.g. special offers, customer loyalty schemes, including how long they are valid for
- the need to take the initiative in communicating with customers in various ways (e.g. responding to complaints and recognising when customers have special requirements) as well as the most appropriate communication method for the communication (e.g. email or phone).

62. Communicating with customers

Learner response. Your answer should show awareness of how different types of communication are appropriate at different times. For example:
- Use the preferred method of communication for the customer, e.g. if they left a voicemail, phone them back or if they emailed, reply to their email.
- Communications should always be clear and professional to maintain the reputation of the business or organisation.
- Email is best if the customer needs large amounts of information, such as a class timetable or payment form.

- Speaking directly to the customer, face-to-face or on the telephone, may be most appropriate to explain a particular situation or deliver a short message.
- Remember body language contributes to communication in face-to-face situations so messages delivered by other means are more easily misinterpreted as they don't have visual clues to back them up.
- Respond to customer complaints calmly and fairly, without getting defensive or allocating blame, even if you don't agree with the complaint.

63. Financing a business

Learner response. Ways to avoid cashflow problems could include:
- budgeting in advance of spending
- writing down everything bought in a week and analysing it to identify where cost savings could be made, e.g. not buying a takeaway coffee every day or bringing own lunch instead of buying it
- saving up for more expensive items by not spending as much money on non-essentials for a short time, e.g. not making impulse purchases, not browsing online shopping sites, socialising at home
- finding an additional source of income, such as a part-time job.

64. Financial records

Answers could include:
- It is a legal requirement to keep some types of records.
- It is necessary for producing an accurate tax return.
- It enables a business to be aware of its financial position, and to make business decisions accordingly.
- It allows a business to have a snapshot of its cashflow in real time.
- It prevents issues when inspectors wish to view the records.
- It enables transparency and allows processes to run smoothly.
- It helps the business to be aware of its debts and to plan how to pay them.
- It helps the business to be aware of what money is owed, and how to claim it.
- It is reassuring for staff to know that robust financial processes are in place and that they are likely to be paid on time.

65. Trends in the sports and active leisure industry: technology, media and social media

Learner response. Your answer should cover factors particularly relevant to social media such as:
- public reactions/reviews, good and bad, affect reputation and brand
- increased brand awareness
- customer service when responding to complaints (and praise)
- instant two-way communication
- visual communication gives an extra dimension
- viral vs transient content
- company needs to keep supplying new content.

66. Trends in the sports and active leisure industry: participation and spectator numbers

Learner response. Your answer should cover how the businesses could take advantage of:
- the influence of the media, including social media
- changes in national participation rates for different activities
- changes in participation and spectator numbers.

67. Developing products and services to take advantage of trends

Learner response. Your answer should take into account:
Benefits
- Improvements and diversification of products, services and customer experience.
- Business growth – development of new target markets, offering USPs.
- Improved reputation.

Risks
- Failing to meet customer needs.
- Failing to anticipate competitor activities.
- Failing to achieve a return on investment.

68. Your Unit 22 set task

Learner response.

69. Getting started with research

Learner response. Your answer should include information about:
- facilities
- products and services
- business operations
- demographics of clients.

70. Reviewing sources

Learner response. Your answer should analyse the reliability of the information found and assess whether it adequately answers:
- why?
- who?
- where?
- what?
- how?

You should also suggest other authoritative sources of data such as professional-society, government or sports-body websites and surveys.

71. Making notes (1)

Learner response. Your spidergram legs could include the following areas:
- Customer demographics
- Description of operations
- Financial data
- Business aims or objectives
- Mission statements
- Customer testimonies
- Product and service updates
- Recent news
- How the business markets itself

Possible sources of information include:
- Company website
- Promotional material
- Annual report
- Social media
- Office for National Statistics

72. Making notes (2)

Learner response. Your answer should compare:
- size of business
- location of business
- roles of staff
- facilities and equipment
- types of products and services offered
- target demographic
- types of membership
- payment plans and price structures.

73. Reviewing business information (1)

1 The business's overheads are really only equipment replacement and administration. Most obviously, the key advantage is the lack of facilities to maintain and service, and there is no need to pay bills such as rent, services or buildings and contents insurance.

2 Social media feeds can be accessed by all, and using well-established media such as Twitter means that organisations like schools can have direct access. The use of LinkedIn as a business tool is also appropriate for this business as it enables it to maintain a professional method of contact and to feed updates as a professional rather than a personal interaction.

3 The business could look to expand in the following ways:
   • Invest in a simple storage facility for canoes and equipment, without amenities. This would potentially remove the need for a van and provide a net saving.
   • Closer partnerships with other local clubs/facilities so that sports like football and athletics can offer multi-sport experiences potentially in school holidays.
   • School membership and incentives: many similar facilities offer support in the assessment for tutoring in outdoor and adventurous activities education modules; Next Generation could also do this.
   • Expand marketing to include non-traditional formats such as Groupon.

74. Reviewing business information (2)

Learner response. Your answer could include the following points:
• The business's customer base is limited. Depending wholly on schools and local authorities is risky in the event of a policy change or budget cut.
• Its lack of facilities could limit its growth.
• It has a strong, low-cost communications strategy with schools but it is unclear whether it also has effective communication with individual members.
• It is in a large town with an untapped market of adults, offering the chance to diversify during quieter times of day and certain periods.
• It has links to local sports clubs – these could be exploited further via partnerships or joint events.
• It is unclear how many members and regular individual attendances it has, making it difficult to assess its income.

75. Business model analysis: SWOT

Learner response. Your answer could cover:

Opportunities
• The business gets free help in the form of unpaid staff.
• Volunteers may have diverse and useful skills and experience that paid staff do not have.
• Volunteers may be enthusiastic and do a good job because of their passion for the activity or motivation for completing an award or qualification.

Threats
• As they are not paid, volunteers cannot be expected to give as much time as may be required, or to take on many responsibilities.
• Volunteers may not be as reliable as paid staff.
• Volunteers with jobs, or who are learners, are only available at certain times of the day.

76. Business model analysis: PESTLE

Learner response. There is no one right answer, but it's important that you provide realistic justifications for your decision.

77. Making recommendations

Learner response. Your answer should take into account concerns of sole traders. For example, a sole trader could improve their business by:
• finding staff/specialist skills to support them
• balancing income with time available, e.g. maximising current quiet times by targeting new markets
• targeting specific demographics that may be interested in archery tag
• diversifying their offer, to mitigate the risk of archery tag's popularity being fleeting
• developing new marketing strategies.

78. Justifying your recommendations

Learner response. Your answer should include:
• a clear relationship between the recommendation and its justification
• use of evidence to back up arguments
• acknowledgement of the wider sporting context, including factors such as business growth, target markets, risks and trends
• logical thinking
• technical terms where appropriate.

Notes

Notes

Notes

Notes

Notes